Preface

To All Mennonite and Reformed Churches

'Mennonites and Reformed in Dialogue' grows out of a day of consultation in Strasbourg, France, more than one year ago. Convened by the Mennonite World Conference (MWC) and the World Alliance of Reformed Churches (WARC), Mennonite and Reformed representatives gathered to ask if the time had come to look afresh at our relations with one another and our common calling to confess the Lordship of Christ in a broken world. They concluded that the time has indeed come — and they issued an appeal for dialogue beginning at the local level.

We support that appeal. We urge Mennonite and Reformed Churches to enter into or deepen dialogue with one another. In order for that to happen, we suggest that local or regional church leaders invite Mennonite and Reformed Christians to meet and converse. Let us listen to one another and talk together about our common roots and history, our unresolved differences, and our mission as churches of Christ in the world today. Where it is not possible for Mennonite and Reformed to meet personally, we encourage each to become more familiar with the other through study of this booklet.

The booklet provides resource and study materials for conversations. We hope that it will prompt and facilitate exchange and learning. We believe that those people who already have some theological and historical background will find reading the booklet useful preparation for the encounters; others will likely find parts of it difficult to understand! In congregational and parish settings, therefore, leaders may want to summarize the materials, lift out key issues and some important questions.

MWC and WARC would like to be informed of local and regional initiatives. In approximately two years we will report the development and result of these conversations. At that time also, we will consider appropriate next steps. Please send information on Mennonite and Reformed encounters in your locale or region to the MWC or the WARC:

Mennonite World Conference 528 E. Madison St. Lombard, IL 60148 USA	World Alliance of Reformed Churches 150, route de Ferney 1211 Geneva 20 SWITZERLAND

Signed:

Ross T. Bender President Mennonite World Conference	Allan Boesak President World Alliance of Reformed Churches
Paul N. Kraybill Executive Secretary Mennonite World Conference	Edmond Perret General Secretary World Alliance of Reformed Churches

Introduction

Beyond Brokenness into God's New Creation

Over July 17-18, 1984, representatives of Reformed and Mennonite churches met in Strasbourg, France, for a day of consultation. They gathered to ask if the time had come for Mennonite and Reformed Christians to look afresh at their relationship to one another. They parted sensing a common call to live under the Lordship of Christ in a changing, divided and threatened world.

The Strasbourg encounter grew out of another consultation, March 5, 1983, held in the place where the two traditions first arose and separated more than 450 years ago — Zurich, Switzerland. On that occasion, delegates of the World Alliance of Reformed Churches (WARC) and of the Baptist World Alliance (BWA) met to celebrate ten years of dialogue. At their request, several Mennonites were present to comment on the significance of the Reformed/Baptist dialogue from the Mennonite point of view. The day of discussion and fellowship culminated in Reformed, Baptists and Mennonites joining together in a public service of confession and communion in the cathedral. After reflection on the events in Zurich, the WARC Executive Committee proposed to the Mennonite World Conference (MWC) a Reformed/Mennonite exchange. MWC agreed to the proposal, inviting Mennonites from several of its constituent churches to meet Reformed delegates in Strasbourg.

Discussion in Strasbourg centred on issues rooted in the history of the Mennonite/Reformed Relations, today's new situation and the possibility of renewed dialogue between Mennonites and Reformed.

THE HISTORY

Mennonite and Reformed Christians meet each other as members of churches with common roots and related stories. In addition to their grounding in biblical and early Christian history, both are rooted in the movement of reform which wanted to bring about renewal of the European church in the sixteenth century. Indeed, some have called the Reformed and Mennonite traditions 'twin sisters'. After all, both claim events of the 1520's in Switzerland and South Germany as foundational. For example, the Zurich Anabaptists — whose heirs are found among today's Mennonites — were literally friends and students of Huldrych Zwingli, one of the fathers of the Reformed tradition. They read the same Bible. They spoke the same theological language. Together they intended to call the Church to live anew in obedience to the unique Lordship of Christ. Later, and in other places too, these two theological

3

currents — Anabaptist and Reformed — were regularly interrelated as neither of them was with other forms of Protestantism.

It is hardly surprising, therefore, that a review of Mennonite and Reformed histories reveals agreement on important issues of Christian faith and practice. From the earliest days in Zurich both traditions have held to the fundamental principles of the Reformation. *Sola scriptura:* Scripture alone is the rule and norm of revelation. *Sola gratia:* God's grace, in Christ and by the Spirit, is the only source of salvation. *Sola fide:* justification is given by faith alone in Christ, apart from any merit or works.

In addition, it has been characteristic of both theologies to underline the importance of sanctification as well as its interrelatedness to justification: 'To be a Christian is not to talk about Christ, but to walk as he walked' (Zwingli). Here, faith in Christ means obedience to him — in the public as well as the private dimension of the Christian's life. Further, both traditions — each in its own way — have placed special emphasis on the church as community: a community opposed to sacramentalism and ritualism; a community committed to build relations and structures for mutual support and discipline.

In spite of these common roots and perspectives, the history of Mennonite and Reformed relations has been marked by unresolved differences. Classically the debate has centered on issues like the nature of the church, its mission and its relation to society; the meaning and practice of Christian discipleship; and baptism. Sometimes, too, the person and the work of Jesus Christ as well as the relationship of Spirit and Word have been subjects of disagreement.

Underlying many of these divergences have been different applications of fundamental Reformation principles. For example, the early Anabaptists — unlike the fathers of the Reformed tradition — applied the principle of *sola fide* not only to justification, but also to epistemology. The words and work of Jesus rather than human reason provide normative guidance in *all* areas of the Christian life, including that of social ethics.

Similarly, the principle of *sola scriptura* has often been applied differently. Though it is held in both traditions that the Bible can be understood only in and through Christ, the relation of the Old Testament to the New Testament has been seen differently. In the Reformed tradition, with its emphasis on the unity of old and new covenants, all of the Bible stood on the same level. The Old Testament, as much as the New, is a source of valid models for Christian faith and practice. In the Mennonite tradition, where the old covenant is understood as promise and the new as fulfilment, emphases are placed on the new, which become examples for faith and practice. Where the New Testament gives a new model the old one has been superseded. For example, Jesus alone, and not Joshua or Josiah, is the model for Christian life in the world.

As early as the 1520's differences had appeared and resulted in division. It has been said that the last real opportunity to reach early agreement on the basic differences was an encounter in Strasbourg late in 1526 between leading representatives of the two tendencies. Soon after that 'interchurch' conversation broke off, it became clear that Reformed and Anabaptist-Mennonites would live in separation and, too often, in antagonism.

As time passed, obstacles to Reformed/Mennonite dialogue on the basic differences arose. Reformed and other Christians attempted to crush the Anabaptist movement through persecution and banishment. Reformed confessions of faith condemned Anabaptists. Anabaptist-Mennonites, a suffering minority, withdrew from contact with the world and other believers. Over the years, Mennonite and Reformed understandings of authority in the church, as well as their patterns for discerning and acting on God's will, continued to develop in divergent ways. Then, too, diversity and differences *within* each tradition grew in time. All of these factors have hindered growth in understanding and agreement.

The Situation Today

But history, with its memory of interrelatedness and schism, agreements and disagreements, is not the whole Reformed and Mennonite story. Today is a new situation.

Between the two Strasbourg encounters — in 1526 where the initial exchange broke off, and in 1984 where representatives convened to ask if the dialogue could begin afresh — the context for conversation has changed. The world in which Mennonite and Reformed Christians live has changed. The setting for the sixteenth century was Europe, because that is where Reformed and Mennonites were located; today both are scattered around the world, neighbors in a variety of cultural environments. The debate took place in the world of European Christendom with its alliances to established church and civil powers; today both Reformed and Mennonite live primarily as minorities in non-Christian and sometimes hostile settings. Whereas the initial conversations took place in the context of a struggle for the renewal of the Church; today the context is the struggle for the survival of human life.

And not only has the world changed; the churches themselves have changed. Through the centuries both Reformed and Mennonite churches have developed and evolved, sometimes in directions not dictated by their theological points of origin. In this new situation the historical debate is transformed. Old issues appear in a new light. New issues appear.

Participants in the Strasbourg encounter agreed that changes in church and world both reinforce the need for and open up new possibilities for Reformed/Mennonite conversations on important

View of Zurich, painted by Hans Leu (ca. 1500); to the left the Grossmünster, to the right the Wasserkirche and behind the Wellenberg, the prison tower of the city (Schweizerisches Landesmuseum Zürich).

issues of Christian faith and practice. Their list of such issues included: the authority of Scripture; the relation of Word and Spirit; the nature of the Church, including models of membership, mutual support and discipline; the mission of the Church in today's world, particularly its relation to the 'powers' (political, social, economic, media); war and peace; violence and non-violence; the shape of Christian discipleship; the meaning and practice of baptism; eschatology.

As Mennonites and Reformed meet and converse with one another, we may find that the traditional confessional boundaries are shifting. Some Reformed Christians take positions on specific issues which Zwingli or Calvin did not take. Some Mennonites hold views which Sattler or Menno did not hold. Some Mennonites and Reformed may feel more spiritual kinship with members of the other church than with members of their own. While certain aspects of these changes could complicate the dialogue, others will enhance it. For example:

A Call To Obedience

While conversation between Christians is important in its own right, it is not an end in itself. Renewed Mennonite and Reformed discussion could lead to the conclusion that the time has come for common commitment and action in specific areas of Christian life and practice. Through the centuries Reformed and Mennonite Christians have confessed the Lordship of Christ over both Church and world. Now the question is: what does obedience to Him mean for Reformed and Mennonite churches today? What does it mean for us in response to the call for Christian unity? Has the time come for Mennonites and Reformed, as twin sisters in the Christian faith, to address the wider church jointly on matters of common concern?

What does obedience to Jesus Christ mean for us today in response to the call for common witness in a non-Christian world? Could Mennonites and Reformed make again, as we did in Zurich more than 450 years ago, a common commitment to Christian witness where Christ's lordship is not recognized? And what does obedience mean for us today in response to the call from the world for peace? Might we join together to make peace non-violently in a world of violence, hunger, injustice and non-respect of human rights?

Debate and Conversation at the Local Level

This booklet is offered to Mennonite and Reformed churches around the world in the conviction that the time has indeed come for us to look afresh at our relationship to each other and our common calling to follow Christ in church and world. It is our hope that the booklet will prompt and facilitate renewed conversation in our worldwide fellowships on these matters.

Theological and practical considerations suggest that the conversation begin at the local level. Our common commitment to the church as community points in this direction. The plurality of local cultural and historical contexts in which Mennonites and Reformed meet today points in the same direction. Mennonite/Reformed relations — the areas of agreement and disagreement, the extent of fellowship or cooperation already established — vary from setting to setting. Each situation calls for its own agenda.

The World Alliance of Reformed Churches and Mennonite World Conference would greatly appreciate being kept informed of local conversations and the Spirit's leading in this dialogue. (A procedure for this is suggested in the preface.) Where we encounter one another with a common commitment to Scripture as normative and an openness to mutual correction, we can expect to be led beyond our brokenness into God's new creation.

Who are the Mennonites today?

CORNELIUS J. DYCK

The Mennonites are the closest descendants of the Anabaptists of the sixteenth century. Increasing numbers of Mennonites worldwide cannot trace their genealogical roots back to sixteenth century Europe, but spiritually and theologically they rightfully claim this heritage. Many Mennonites are still ethnically part of the Germanic lineage, but in Christ a new people of God is arising, in a large variety of global contexts, who are indeed one family as Mennonites in the sense of Acts 2 and Ephesians 2.

The Mennonites were first called *Menists,* or Mennonites, by Countess Anna of Friesland in 1541, after Menno Simons (1496-1561), to distinguish them, as peaceful settlers whom she welcomed in her lands, from other more revolutionary groups. They were also called *Anabaptists,* a pejorative term at the time, because they insisted on forming congregations composed only of persons who had been baptized on confession of faith.

Historical Facts and Interpretations

People cannot know or describe themselves apart from their history. This may be particularly true of many western Mennonites, for whom their history is part of their theology and identity. A theology of discipleship, for example, is difficult to describe except in the concrete historical situation. The experience of terrible suffering on the part of thousands of Mennonite forebears in the sixteenth century, to which many martyrologies testify (of which the best known is *Martyrs' Mirror),* has a continuing impact on Mennonite theology, social attitudes, ethics, and even self-awareness. We cannot abruptly break into the present without an understanding of the forces and power of the historical.

Until the later nineteenth century most historians treated the Anabaptists and Mennonites as stepchildren of the Reformation, and few theologians took them seriously. Most Mennonites, except for the Dutch (who call themselves *Doopsgezinde* — baptism-minded), did not care much about what the 'world' thought or said about them, and were content to be left alone. But when the actual documents of Anabaptism began to be published early in the twentieth century, historians, sociologists, theologians, and the Mennonites themselves, began to develop strong interest in the subject. The image of the Anabaptists and Mennonites changed so completely, that it seemed to many too good to be true.

The Mennonite story as it was told until about 1960 began in Zurich, Switzerland, and centered around the Reformer Huldrych Zwingli (1484-1531). Through debates arranged by him and the city council, numerous reforms were introduced into church life in the area. Soon a circle of students and other admirers gathered around him, including Conrad Grebel (c.1489-1526) and Felix Mantz (c.1498-1527) who were to become future Anabaptists. But for Grebel and Mantz the reforms came too slowly and did not go far enough. They also believed Zwingli had changed his mind on baptism and on the nature of the church. He seemed to be content to let the Great Council of 200 in Zurich decide issues which they, his critics, thought the Bible had already decided. The rift between Zwingli and his students increased. On January 17, 1525 the Great Council decreed that all infants should be baptized within eight days, defaulting parents to be banished.

This precipitated a crisis within the Grebel circle. At one of their Bible study sessions on January 21, 1525 a number of them baptized each other and held a communion service. Persecution and death soon followed, but the number of believers increased far more rapidly than they were killed. The Anabaptists were mostly popular with the people because they talked of a truly reformed church, renewed in doctrine and, especially, in practice. Michael Sattler (c.1490-1527), a former Benedictine turned Anabaptist, convened a meeting at Schleitheim in 1527 after failing to win Bucer in Strasbourg to his points of view. A 'confession' of seven articles commonly known as the *Brotherly Union* was drafted. Sattler was martyred soon after, but the articles became a landmark for the new movement.

Thus, according to this historiography, the Zwinglian reformation was completed and the true church restored in Anabaptism. Even more, according to the American church historian Roland H. Bainton, three values considered central to a democratic society today — the voluntary church, the separation of church and state, and religious liberty — were first articulated by the Anabaptists. The 'Left Wing of the Reformation' (Bainton), or the 'Free Church' (Littell), the 'Radical Reformation' (Williams), or more recently the 'Believers' Church',[2] had finally come into its own. From Strasbourg, Melchior Hoffman (c. 1495-1543) carried the message to Emden and the Lowlands. Munster and other radical episodes lay completely outside the boundaries of this history of the movement. It was, in fact, in opposition to the radical developments in the Lowlands that Menno began his work in 1536.

During recent decades this historiography has been modified. New sources have been discovered, younger social historians have taken different approaches and, through the interest of Marxist scholars, Thomas Muntzer (1488?-1525), has been given new attention.

Much of this present emphasis awaits the test of time, but its collective impact is important. Wilhelm Reublin, Johannes Brötli and other clerics in the Zurich highlands stirred up the peasants not to pay their tithes and, later, not to baptize their children. Many of these people later became Anabaptists. Balthasar Hubmaier's ministry in Waldshut was not only religious but also socio-political in its implications to the point where it almost appeared to be an Anabaptist territorial church in 1524-25. Albrecht Ritchl's earlier thesis about the monastic nature of Anabaptism has found support in recent research (Snyder). Their Erasmian and ascetic roots have been affirmed (Davis), as have their indebtedness to mysticism (Packull), and the wide diversity of their origins (Stayer, Packull, Deppermann).[3] The boundaries of what and who really was Anabaptist have been so enlarged that some scholars find it difficult to identify any common, normative consensus among them.

What is new in this is:

1) the discovery of numerous social factors leading to a pre-disposition towards Anabaptism by the people around Zurich versus the former purely religious interpretation;

2) the realization that early Anabaptism in Zurich, Strasbourg, and other places was initially non-separatist, seeking the reform of the entire community through legal, socio-political processes;

3) the acknowledgement that much of early Anabaptism was, in fact, revolutionary at certain stages, not only in Munster and the Lowlands, but also in specific movements in Switzerland and South Germany;

4) the very significant influence of Andreas Bodenstein von Karlstadt (1480-1541), both on the Swiss and Dutch streams of the movement.

These historiographical developments modify both the image of historical Anabaptism and the self-image of Mennonites today. The new elements of this genesis need to be absorbed into present Mennonite identity and self-consciousness.

The Hutterites and the Amish

Anabaptism spread from Switzerland and South Germany into the Austrian lands and the Tyrol, but the severity of Austrian persecution under the direction of Archduke Ferdinand, drove large numbers of these new converts into Moravia. By 1527 Nicolsburg was a major center, numbering perhaps as many as 12,000 Anabaptists. Key leaders at that time included Hans Hut (?-1527) and Balthasar Hubmaier (1480?-1528). While both helped significantly to give shape to the community, they differed on many theological issues, and eventually both continued their mission elsewhere.

In 1533 Jacob Hutter (?-1536) became a recognized leader of the Nicolsburg community, thus becoming the actual founder of the

Hutterian Brethren. They were soon known for their practice of community of goods and their intense missionary zeal, as well as for their orderly communal life and skilled craftsmen, who were in great demand far beyond their own community. Hutterite writings of the sixteenth century constitute a rich collection of spiritual and historical literature. Today there are perhaps 12,000 baptized members in a multitude of communities in North America. These communities *(Bruderhof)* are almost completely self-sufficient. All property is held in common and production is also communal. Farming is the primary occupation. Hutterites wear a plain, uniform garb. Television and other modern conveniences are not allowed, but in farming itself the most modern tractors, trucks and other machinery are used. They are Anabaptist in origin and intention to this day. A key spiritual term for them is *Gelassenheit* (yieldedness, surrender), which can come only to those who renounce all private possessions. A small community has recently formed itself in Tokyo with the official blessing of a community in Canada.[4]

A major schism occurred among the Mennonites in Switzerland and Alsace from 1693-97, when Jacob Ammann (1644?-?) became concerned over worldliness and lack of discipline among his people. Excommunications followed and, in spite of serious attempts at reconciliation, the Amish, as they became known, have continued separately to this day. Further divisions continued among them over these same issues. Most Amish live in North America, comprising some 35,000 baptized members.

Like the Hutterian Brethren, the Amish are Anabaptist in origin. Some groups are, in fact, closer to sixteenth century Anabaptist norms than their 'cousins', the Mennonites, today. Amish groups vary among themselves primarily in the degree of accommodation to the 'world'. Most do not use modern conveniences either in the home or in farming, but some groups allow members to own such things as cars and telephones. They have basically retained the dress customs of early eighteenth century Europe. Humility is an important spiritual theme. They care for each other financially and spiritually, including church discipline. They are always ready to help anyone in need. Movies about them like 'Witness' cause them considerable distress.[5]

Migrations

Historically the most significant factor shaping the ethos of the descendants of Swiss and Dutch Anabaptists may have been persecution. This fostered a continuing pilgrim consciousness, and led to many migrations — from Switzerland and the Tyrol to Moravia, as we have seen, as well as to the Palatinate, Hesse, and Poland. From the Netherlands migrations along the North Sea and Baltic coasts began in 1530, leading to large concentrations of settlers in the

12

Danzig (Gdansk) and Vistula River areas. New major movements from this latter area (Prussia) to the Ukraine began in 1787 and continued until 1870. Early, sporadic migrations to North America began in the 1660s, with the first permanent German-Dutch settlement in America established by Mennonites and Quakers at Germantown in 1683. Numerous other migrations followed, the largest being from the Ukraine to the Canadian and American midwest in the 1870s, when some 18,000 persons came, and again in the 1920s, when some 23,000 persons migrated from the Ukraine, primarily to Canada, but also to Paraguay and Brazil.

During World War I the Manitoba (Canada) government insisted that instruction in Mennonite schools be conducted in the English language and that these schools come under provincial educational authorities. This was seen as a threat to their faith by some conservative Mennonites, leading to some migrations from Canada to Mexico and Paraguay in the 1920s, later extending to Bolivia and Central America. These migrations came about because of a sharp church-world dualism which the migrants considered congruent with New Testament faithfulness. The motives of the migrants were often mixed, including social, economic, and other needs. This mobility, in turn, fostered an inner-directed ethnicity, a loss of a sense of mission and, perhaps, a sense of satisfaction, if not pride, at being more faithful than others.

Privilegium was another legacy of this persecution and consequent dualism: beginning with the movement to Russia, and continuing in Canada, Paraguay, and other locations, the migrating groups insisted on specific special privileges for themselves and their descendants in perpetuity, given in writing by the respective governments in advance of their coming. These guarantees included freedom of religion, complete autonomy in all civil, cultural, educational, and economic affairs of the colonies, exemption from military service, the right to use the German and low-German languages, and other stipulations, including the right to brew their own beer, vinegar and brandy. Privileges were sought in the United States only by the migrants of the 1870s from Russia, but they were not granted. Several states, however, did pass legislation favorable to Mennonite interests. Cultural integration and assimilation, albeit to varying degrees, eventually became inevitable in the North American environment and, apparently, more recently also in Russia, but numerous Mennonite enclaves continue to exist in both North and South America. It must also be remembered that in every migration more people stayed than left, but most North American Mennonites, for example, are descendants of those who left.

We have thus far been describing the origin and legacy of Swiss and Dutch Anabaptism. Yet these account for only about half of the Mennonites living today. In 1984 there were approximately

92,700 baptized members in Europe, including the USSR, 101,000 in Canada, and 239,000 in the United States, totaling about 432,700 members. However, many of these are what are sometimes referred to as new Mennonites, or Mennonites by choice (versus Mennonites by parentage). Theologically speaking there are no birthright Mennonites, but in practice sound nurture in church and home as well as the momentum of being born into a Mennonite home have often tended to unite the biological (Swiss and Dutch ethnic heritage) stream with the spiritual. The new Mennonite, on the other hand, joins because of some deep conviction, whether it be peace or believer's baptism or total faith emphasis. Some, of course, also join through marriage to a Mennonite.

Mennonites in Africa, Asia and Latin America

While the Anabaptists were, in fact and by definition, the only missionaries of the Reformation, the intense enthusiasm of the first generation had largely spent itself by the time of Menno's death in 1561, hastened by persecution and diaspora. The Hutterian Brethren continued their witness to about 1600. From that time on most overt mission activity ceased among Mennonites until the mid-nineteenth century when the influence of Pietism was felt in southern Russia. Dutch Mennonites founded a missionary society in 1847, and the new missionary interest of other denominations brought similar stirrings to Mennonites in North America. It was late nineteenth century before the latter recovered something of the spirit of the first generation.

In North America a slow beginning was made among native Americans in the 1880s, followed by work in India, Argentina, China, and in ever widening circles into all the world. It was not until after World War II, however, and the decline of colonialism, that full autonomy became a reality in most Mennonite missionary situations.

With a global 1984 total of 730,000 Mennonites, it is obvious that those members coming out of the original Swiss and Dutch movements today comprise only somewhat more than half of the worldwide membership. The mission activities of the Mennonites have added over 300,000 members in Africa, Asia, Latin and North America, where are located some of the fastest growing congregations and conferences.

Of the eleven countries in Africa where organized Mennonite life exists, Zaire has the largest number (66,400) and Burkina Faso the fewest (13). The approximate membership total in Africa in 1984 was 107,300.

Congregations and conferences in Asia include the following: Hong Kong 35 members, India 44,000, Indonesia 63,000, Japan 2,700, the Philippines 2,500, Taiwan 1,200, and Vietnam 150, for an approximate total of 113,600 members, plus one congregation in Australia.

Some 76,300 members live and work in Latin America, with a presence in almost every nation. This latter figure includes Dutch-Russian ethnic Mennonites who migrated there from Canada. All of the statistics given include baptized members only.

In recent decades the most visible and dynamic expression of global Mennonite unity have been Mennonite World Conference (MWC) assemblies held every five or six years. In these sessions both unity and diversity, theological as well as cultural, have been celebrated. Here is the most creative global forum Mennonites possess for dialogue, worship, and social meeting even though North American Mennonites have tended to be over-represented.

MWC began in Europe in 1925. In keeping with Mennonite congregational polity, the meetings are given to discussion, fellowship and worship, rather than to the drafting of resolutions binding upon its members. There is, of couse, a sense of the meeting, and many small group discussions, but at the 1984 MWC Strasbourg sessions, for example, no statements of concern came before the entire assembly on issues like nuclear armaments, Central America, or the Middle East. Still, it is in such MWC assemblies that Mennonites feel most equal.

Mennonite Doctrinal Emphases

Differences among Mennonites worldwide, involving 52 or more countries and cultures, as they do, lie more in the area of practice than of doctrine, and in degrees of emphases given to specific con-victions. The Apostles' Creed is not widely used in Mennonite worship, but its affirmations would constitute a baseline of agreement with Christians everywhere.

While Mennonites are non-creedal and affirm the Bible as their final authority, numerous confessions have been written by them throughout their history. Chief among these are the *Brotherly Union* (Schleitheim, 1527) and the *Dordrecht Confession of Faith* (1632). The latter was drafted first by Adrian Cornelis, minister of the Flemish Mennonite church in Dordrecht, later revised and signed by 51 leaders of the Flemish and Frisian Mennonites as an instrument of union between them.[6] It is now recognized that Schleitheim, especially the church-world dualism of article four, is as much rooted in Sattler's monastic background as in fresh biblical studies, but the articles had a formative influence significant enough for John Calvin to write a refutation, *Brieve Instruction,* in 1544.[7] Its influence on American Mennonitism was largely covert, but important. The *Dordrecht Confession* was adopted by the Mennonites in Pennsyl-vania in 1725. The articles on footwashing, excommunication, and shunning continue to make it appealing particularly to conservative groups in North America. Conversations are now in process between the Mennonite Church (MC) and the General Conference Mennonite Church (GCMC) about writing a new, joint confessional statement. In the same way groups around the world have written their own confessions over the years, as they were needed for didactic purposes, and to promote unity. A collection of global Mennonite confessions of faith is now available.[8]

1. *Biblical Authority and Interpretation.* Most Mennonites believe the Bible to be the the Word of God, written under the inspiration of the Holy Spirit. Some insist that the adjective infallible be used, as in 'infallible guide to faith and life'. Most Mennonites agree with the Anabaptist Marpeck (d. 1556), that the Old Testament is promise, the New Testament fulfilment. Christ's life, death, and resurrection constitute the watershed of history. Christ is the center of Scripture. Where the New Testament gives a new commandment the old law has been superseded. Only in and through Christ can the true meaning of Scripture be understood. Yet this understanding must be illuminated by the Spirit. Word and Spirit must not be separated, and will never contradict each other, but neither will the Spirit give a new revelation not contained in Scripture.

Several other phrases are frequently used by Mennonites today. One his 'epistemology of obedience', that is, we understand God's Word and will best when we live according to what we already know of his will. To be sure, grace is often given precisely in our disobedience, but obedience opens the door to understanding. Another phrase used is 'hermeneutical community', which means that a text is best understood within the context of the congregation. This does not rule out the trained exegete, but stresses that the fruit of such scholarship is to be tested in the circle of believers. Careful use of the historical-critical method is affirmed, provided it is helpful to the church and theologically accountable. The social world of the text and of the interpreter are both to be taken seriously. Many Mennonites, however, might be more comfortable with Menno's statement that 'the Word is plain, and needs no interpretation', that is, it needs to be obeyed.

2. *The Nature of the Church.* The church, or congregation, is that group of people for whom Christ is truly Saviour and Lord, who daily seek to follow his teaching and example, and who live in a vital relationship with each other. This means that a conscious, mature decision has been made by every member in choosing to belong to this fellowship, and that baptism has been requested and received as the sign of a new covenant. This is the ideal. In practice the

16

problem of inherited faith remains. However, during the past several decades the impact of 'new' Mennonites in congregations everywhere, coupled with a strong nurture program, and some influence from the charismatic movement, has frequently led to a real recovery of first generation zeal.

The sixteenth century ideal of the autonomy of the church from the state continues to be affirmed in theory. In fact, however, both democratic and totalitarian regimes (of right and left) are eroding the boundaries. In North America and Europe many Mennonites are deeply involved in the political process, holding office even at the national cabinet level. It is argued that this is at the individual rather than congregational level, but there is no doubt that many younger Mennonites do not see themselves as a quiet and withdrawn minority, but actively participate in the discussion of great international issues like war, peace, hunger, and justice. This conscientization has also been the cause of serious tensions among and within congregations.

The Mennonite Church is still a suffering church today in parts of Asia, Africa, and Latin America, though no new *Martyrs' Mirror* (1660) has been written. In Western Europe and North America it is primarily members of minority groups who still suffer the violence of unjust social and economic structures; most of the rest enjoy a comfortable middle class way of life. But there is also much compassion for the oppressed among the latter group, and many efforts are being made to 'set the captives free'.

Mennonites observe two ordinances, believers' baptism and the Lord's Supper. The latter is celebrated at least two to four times annually. In some congregations the love feast, involving a meal and fellowship around a table before the bread and wine is passed, is observed. The Supper is seen as a memorial to the sacrificial death of Christ and his glorious resurrection, a foretaste of the great banquet of the Lamb to which believers look forward. Baptism is the outer witness to an inner faith commitment. Pouring is the dominant mode of baptism, but immersion is also practiced. Footwashing is practiced in some congregations.

Worship services among Mennonites are sermon centered. A simple, almost austere, liturgy surrounds the gospel proclamation. Time for Sunday morning education and Bible study classes for children and adults is still taken in many congregations worldwide. Women are finding increasing acceptance in Mennonite pulpits in North America, and some congregations in the Third World, as they have long been accepted in some parts of western Europe. Small group meetings for Bible study and fellowship seem to be increasing as supplements to the Sunday morning worship experience. These groups often also function as a means of evangelism and ecumenical witness.

3. *The Meaning and Practice of Discipleship.* For Mennonites historically, and today also, Christianity without discipleship is Christianity without Christ. Ethics is part of the Good News in Jesus Christ. Grace is necessary for discipleship rather than being antithetical to it. The Second Adam, Christ, has undone the damage of the first Adam, making possible a gradual transformation of the disciples' life into the image of Christ himself. This is the process of sanctification and holiness.

This is a pilgrim motif. The disciple lives in the world and seeks to serve humankind. What sometimes appears as withdrawal is actually the world separating itself from the disciple. Thus numerous intentional communities have arisen from North America to Tokyo, in which economic sharing is freely practiced, but secular individualism feels threatened by this intimacy and call to trust. Again, love is seen as so central to discipleship that non-resistance and loving the enemy become ethical absolutes. Mennonites in totalitarian situations consider this a democratic luxury, but it is amazing how much love is being lived out daily under oppressive regimes. Meanwhile, a fair number of Mennonites in democratic societies consider non-resistance socially and morally irresponsible. The range of practice among Mennonites is wide on this issue, from refusal to register for military service in the United States and active opposition to nuclear armaments production, including European Mennonite opposition to the placement of nuclear missiles, to complete cooperation with the military by other Mennonites in North America and around the world.

A problem Mennonites still struggle with in this connection is legalism and perfectionism. Universality is sacrificed for intensity, but a violin string can be tightened only so far before it breaks. Lacking in many situations is that dimension of divine grace which keeps the string from breaking. In addition to economics and pacifism, Mennonite discipleship has become more sensitive in the area of justice — locally, nationally, and globally. Locally, for example, the Victim and Offender Reconciliation Program (VORP), which works with the local courts and police in bringing reconciliation between victims of a crime and the offenders, is widely practiced in North America. Nationally, Mennonites in North America and Europe have been demonstrating against the production of nuclear weapons, for example, and have gone to jail for it. Internationally, Mennonites have gone beyond relief activities, for example, to be present in Nicaragua, as well as to initiate dialogue with governments in Washington and Ottawa on a variety of crucial issues. From the era of asking governments for special privileges (Russia, North America, South America) Mennonites are finding courage to be advocates on behalf of the poor and oppressed — from native Canadians to Central American refugees to ecological concerns and

18

the global exploitation by some multinational corporations. 'What does it mean to follow Jesus?' is being asked with new intensity by many Mennonites today.

A final area of discipleship concern for Mennonites is personal ethics. Ranging from abortion to homosexuality, from divorce to promiscuity, from alcohol and drugs to practicing a personal life of prayer and contemplation, these are the the kinds of issues Mennonites discuss, face, and cope with daily. In a study of five Mennonite groups in America it was learned that about four-fifths of the members could identify a specific conversion experience; daily personal prayer ranged from a low of 73 percent in one conference to a high of 82 in another; 85 percent considered sexual intercourse before marriage as always wrong; fewer than two percent of the membership have experienced divorce or separation. A church-world dualism, pacifism, nonswearing of oaths, and church discipline were affirmed by a range of from 60 to 80 percent, depending upon the conference. It may be assumed that the record of Mennonites in Asia, Africa, and South America would be stronger.

Discipleship has often taken the shape of service and relief in society. Mennonites have tried to help the poor, giving of their time and skills to alleviate human need, and healing the sick. The emergency relief committee founded by the Dutch Mennonites in 1725, is still active. In 1920 the Mennonite Central Committee (MCC) was founded for similar reasons in North America and continues today with strong congregational support, having a budget of many millions of dollars annually and some 900 — 1,000 workers in the field. So, also, agencies were established in Europe (IMO), in India (MCSFI), and almost every place where Mennonites live and work. It may be that this activity is rooted in an attempt to strengthen the Mennonite image in society, but it nevertheless remains a significant mark of discipleship.

Mennonites and the Ecumenical Movement

Most Mennonites feel a spiritual unity with all believers who acknowledge Jesus Christ as Saviour and Lord, and who seek the way of discipleship. On the other hand, they are generally afraid of 'entangling alliances' which might compromise their life and witness. In North America, for example, the General Conference Mennonite Church, which had joined the Federal Council of Churches in 1908, left it in 1917 — because of the militarist spirit in member congregations of the FCC — and has not joined any ecumenical body since. Two smaller North American Mennonite conferences have joined the National Association of Evangelicals (NAE). The Dutch and North German conferences are members of the World Council of Churches (WCC). Mennonites do hear those who urge that they are needed at national and WCC levels, but the level of trust needed for this to happen is simply lacking at the congregational and, perhaps, conference levels. The radical congregationalism of most Mennonite bodies certainly contributes to these feelings also.

Mennonite ecclesial emphasis is on the local congregation. They would tend to say that the real church is the local congregation, that the universal church is a spiritual rather than structural goal or concept. The church must be visible, the body of believers together. Organizations and institutions are not the church, though Mennonites have many of both. But Mennonites are increasingly open to dialogue with other Christian groups — to learn from them, and to help fulfil the dominical prayer of John 17 'that they may all be one'. Who knows how the Holy Spirit may yet lead this small group of God's people?

FOOTNOTES

[1] *The Bloody Theater or Martyrs' Mirror of the Defenseless Christians.* Scottdale, Pa., Mennonite Publishing House, 1950, pp. 1157. A translation of the 1660 Dutch original compiled by Thieleman J. van Braght, Mennonite pastor. He in turn drew heavily on *Het Offer des Heeren* (The Sacrifice of the Lord) which had been published anonymously in 1562. This collection of Anabaptist martyr stories may in turn have been inspired by a German collection of Reformed and other martyrs compiled in Strasbourg by Ludwig Rabus in 1552, and translated into Dutch by a Reformed minister, Adriaan van Haemsted, in 1559 in Antwerp. Part 1 of the *Martyrs' Mirror,* consisting of 354 pages, is given to the suffering of *defenseless* Christians through the ages, beginning with the early church and continuing to the sixteenth century. Part 2 is given to accounts of Anabaptist martyrs. The significance of Part 1 lies in part in the compilers' intention to show the continuity of the faithful from the time of Christ into the seventeenth century. For discussions of the *Martyrs' Mirror* and the suffering motif in Anabaptism see Ethelbert Stauffer, 'The Anabaptist Theology of Martyrdom'. *Mennonite Quarterly Review,* XIX (July, 1945), Gerald C. Studer, 'A History of the Martyrs' Mirror', *MQR,* XXII (July, 1948), pp. 163-179; Alan F. Kreider, ' "The Servant Is Not Greater Than His Master" : The Anabaptists and the Suffering Church', *MQR,* LVIII (January, 1984), pp. 5-29; Cornelius J. Dyck, 'The Suffering Church in Anabaptism', *MQR,* LIX (January, 1985), pp. 5-23.

[2] Roland H. Bainton, 'The Anabaptist Contribution to History' in *The Recovery of the Anabaptist Vision.* Edited by Guy F. Hershberger. Scottdale, Pa.: Herald Press, 1957, pp. 317-326. Franklin H. Littell, *The Free Church.* Boston: Starr King Press, 1957.

George H. Williams, *The Radical Reformation.* Philadelphia: The Westminster Press, 1962. Donald F. Durnbaugh, *The Believers' Church. The History and Character of Radical Protestantism.* New York: The Macmillan Company, 1968.

[3] Hans-Jürgen Goertz (ed.), *Umstrittenes Täufertum 1525-1975.* Göttingen: Vandenhoeck and Ruprecht, 1975. Hans Hillerbrand, 'The Origin of Sixteenth-Century Anabaptism: Another Look', *Archiv für Reformationsgeschichte* (1962), pp. 152-180. James M. Stayer and Werner O. Packull, *The Anabaptists and Thomas Müntzer.* Toronto: Kendall/Hunt Publishing Company, 1980. Kenneth R. Davis, *Anabaptism and Asceticism.* Scottdale: Herald Press, 1974. Claus-Peter Clasen, *Anabaptism: A Social History, 1525-1618.* Ithaca: Cornell University Press, 1972. Hans-Jürgen Goertz, *Die Täufer: Geschichte and Deutung.* Munchen: Verlag C. H. Beck, 1980. Werner O. Packull, *Mysticism and the Early South German-Austrian Anabaptist Movement, 1525-1531.* Scottdale: Herald Press, 1977. C. Arnold Snyder, *The Life and Thought of Michael Sattler.* Scottdale: Herald Press, 1984. James M. Stayer, Werner O. Packull, and Klaus Deppermann, 'From Monogenesis to Polygenesis: The Historical Discussion of Anabaptist Origins', *MQR,* XLIX (April, 1975), pp. 83-121. Abraham Friesen, 'Wilhelm Zimmermann and Friedrich Engels: Two Sources of the Marxist Interpretation of Anabaptism', *MQR,* LV (July, 1981), pp. 240-254. 'Problems of Anabaptist History: A Symposium', MQR, LIII (July, 1979) the entire issue. And finally, but not least, Calvin A. Pater, *Karlstadt as the Father of the Baptist Movements: The Emergence of Lay Protestantism.* Toronto: University of Toronto Press, 1984.

[4] John A. Hostetler, *Hutterite Society.* Baltimore: Johns Hopkins University Press, 1980.

[5] John A. Hostetler, *Amish Society.* Baltimore: Johns Hopkins University Press, 1974.

[6] John H. Yoder, *The Legacy of Michael Sattler.* Scottdale: Herald Press, 1973, pp. 34-43. John C. Wenger, *Glimpses of Mennonite History and Doctrine.* Scottdale: Herald Press, 1959, pp. 214-228.

[7] John Calvin, *Brieve Instruction pour armer tous bons Fidèles contre les erreurs de la secte commune des anabaptistes* (Geneva, 1544), *Corpus Reformatorum,* ed. C. G. Bretschneider and H. E. Birdseil (Halle, 1834-1869), VII, pp. 45-142.

[8] Howard Loewen (ed.), *One Lord, One Church, One Hope, and One God.* Elkhart, In.: Institute of Mennonite Studies, 1985.

Delegation from the USSR introduced to the World Mennonite Conference in Strasbourg 1984, by the General Secretary Paul Kraybill (right)

The Reformed Family: A Profile

ALAN P.F. SELL

Despite lapses into heterodoxy, pietism and fundamentalism, the Reformed family of churches is best characterized by its quest of the living Word of God made known by the Spirit through the scriptures pondered in fellowship. To be open to this Word is to be *semper reformanda;* it is to be active in mission and witness to a world whose God of grace is sovereign Lord of creation and redemption. These aims unite the historically, theologically, ecclesiologically, culturally, linguistically, and economically diverse Reformed family, whose major means of international fellowship and corporate testimony is the World Alliance of Reformed Churches. This Alliance of 159 member churches in more than 80 lands results from the union in 1970 of the World Presbyterian Alliance (1875) with the International Congregational Council (first meeting 1891, constitution 1948).

The family as a whole subscribes to no one confession of faith; advocates no one ecclesiology; acknowledges no one founder. Nor can a simple list of 'Reformed' doctrines be adumbrated as if these were the exclusive possession of the family. We cannot say that the family originates in the sixteenth century Reformation, for that would be to overlook the Waldensian and Hussite Reformations, which were earlier. Baptismal practice varies, a few older churches and some newer united churches admitting both paedobaptism and believers' baptism as alternatives. Finally, Reformed churches cannot be defined in terms of their relation to the state since while most are free churches a few are established.

In view of this diversity the most satisfactory approach is the inductive. We shall first indicate the elements which go to make up the Reformed family as currently known, and then refer to confessional standards: polity, theology, worship and international bodies.

The Reformed Family

1. *The pre-Reformation strand.* The Italian Waldensian Church looks back to the work of Peter Valdo (12th cent.), who advocated poor and godly living in accordance with the Sermon on the Mount. The Waldensians entered the stream of Swiss Reformed teaching at the Synod of Chanforan (1532), taking their own emphases with them. In the same year the Bohemian Unitas Fratrum, whose earlier inspiration was Jan Hus (c. 1369-1415), and who were currently in dialogue with Luther, published their *Account of Faith*. They too came into the Reformed stream, though in 1533 they urged their Italian friends *'Reformated, habito tum sui ipsius, tum aliorum respecto.'* (Be Reformed, but respect your own heritage and that of others).

2. *The 16th and 17th centuries: Reformers and Puritans.* In 1518 Ulrich Zwingli (1484-1531) was called to Zurich, where he propagated Reformation teaching. At the Marburg Colloquy (1529) he and Luther failed to agree on the last of fifteen articles of faith, Luther holding that Christ was corporally present at the Lord's Supper, Zwingli that he was spiritually present. From this time the Swiss Reformation took its own direction. Zwingli abolished the mass and gave communion in both kinds as a memorial of the death of Christ. On his death Martin Bucer (1491-1551) led the Reformed churches of Switzerland and South Germany. In 1536 Geneva declared for the Reformed faith under the ministry of Farel (1489-1565). Calvin (1509-64), the first edition of whose *Institute* had been published at Basel in 1536, visited Geneva in 1537, and was prevailed upon by Farel to stay. In 1558 Beza (1519-1605) accepted Calvin's invitation to teach at the newly opened Academy; and in 1566 Bullinger (1504-75) published his Second Helvetic Confession.

In France Farel's teacher Lefevre (1450-1536) had espoused Reformed ideas, though hoping for reformation within the Roman Church. His translation of the New Testament into French (1523) was influential. By 1559, when the Confession of La Rochelle was adopted, the French Reformed community counted 2,000 congregations.

John Knox (1505-72), who had lectured in Geneva (1556-9) was instrumental in planting Reformed teaching and presbyterian order in Scotland. Under William the Silent the Netherlanders revolted against Spanish rule, represented locally by the Duke of Alva. After considerable unrest the Seven Provinces, which had already claimed religious liberty under the Treaty of Utrecht (1579), finally broke from Spain and elected Wiliam of Orange Stadtholder for life.

In Germany Lutheran teaching was adopted in Lippe in 1538. Later, Melanchthon's ideas were introduced, and in 1648 the National Church adopted a Reformed confession, while prescribing toleration for Lutherans. In north-west Germany the work (1540-9) of John à Lasco (1499-1560) led to the adoption of the Reformed faith. Elsewhere in Germany the Heidelberg Catechism (1563), whose architects were Ursinus (1534-83) and Olevianus (1536-87), provided the doctrinal link between scattered Reformed churches. In 1884 the Reformierte Bund was founded to foster the Reformed interest and from 1933 onwards most of its members stood with the Confessing Church and were in sympathy with the Barmen Declaration (1934). In the GDR the Reformed Conference unites churches most of which date from the 1780s, and were founded in the wake of the persecution of Reformed Christians in France and the Palatinate.

À Lasco's work in his native Poland led to the introduction of the Reformed polity there, and to the publication of the Polish (Brescz or Radzwill) Bible in 1563. The Transylvanian Mátyás

Dévay (?-c. 1547) came into contact with Zwinglian ideas in Basel (1538), and returned with these to his homeland in 1542. The first Hungarian Reformed Confession was published in 1562; in 1566 the Geneva Catechism was adopted; and in 1567 the Synod of Debrecen adopted the Second Helvetic Confession and the Heidelberg Catechism. Reformed churches have existed in Belgium, Lithuania and elsewhere since the 16th century.

In England many remained unsatisfied with the Anglican Settlement of 1534, which followed Henry VIII's break with Rome, and sought a more thoroughgoing reformation of the church. During the reign of Edward VI increasing links were forged between Cranmer (1489-1556) and such Reformers as Bucer, Peter Martyr (1500-62), and Ochino (1487-1564). The Forty-Two Articles of 1553 thus have a Calvinistic flavor. Edward's reign saw also the rise of the Puritans, among whose leaders was Nicholas Ridley (c. 1500-55). They sought 'pure' worship and church life according to the scriptures, and opposed the 'trappings' of Rome. During the reign of Mary (1553-58), many Puritans were persecuted, exiled, or driven underground. In the reign of Elizabeth I (1558-1603) the drive for religious uniformity under an episcopalian order prompted the Puritans to adopt one of three main positions. There were those who sought a Reformed church on episcopalian lines; those who sought the same, though with presbyterial order; and those who despaired of adequate reform within any kind of established church, and became separatists. These last, including Robert Browne (c. 1550-1633) and the martyrs Henry Barrow (c. 1550-93) and John Greenwood (d.1593) were among the harbingers of Congregationalism. James I (1603-25) declared of the non-episcopalians, 'I will make them conform, or I will harry them out of the land.' Accordingly many separatists fled to Holland, where the Anabaptist air they breathed there left a permanent mark on Congregationalism's understanding of the Church and of its relations to the State, and of freedom under the Spirit.

In 1620 some of the English exiles left Holland and went, with others from England, as pilgrims to the New World. There they were joined by those of Presbyterian and Baptist persuasion. In 1628 Dutch settlers planted their Reformed Church in Manhattan Island. American Presbyterians organised their first Presbytery (Philadelphia) in 1706, and the first General Assembly was held in 1789 under the presidency of John Witherspoon (1722-94).

Meanwhile in England Civil War had broken out (1642-51), Charles I (1625-49) was beheaded, and there followed the Commonwealth and Protectorate (1649-60). Oliver Cromwell (1599-1658) came to power in 1653, and religious freedom was granted to all who professed 'faith in God by Jesus Christ.' With the Restoration of the monarchy (1660) a harsh drive for episcopalian conformity was resumed. At the Great Ejectment (1660-62), when nearly 2,000 clergymen left their livings rather than give their 'unfeigned assent and consent' to the Book of Common Prayer, many Congregationalists and even more Presbyterians came out, the latter having finally forsaken any hope of a Presbyterian establishment in England. The Toleration Act of 1689 gave the right of freedom of worship to dissenters under certain conditions, though Roman Catholics and Unitarians were not included within its provisions.

3. *Evangelical Awakening and Mission.* The Awakening of the second half of the eighteenth century both stimulated English Dissent and American Congregationalism and Presbyterianism and provoked opposition therefrom because of the dislike of 'enthusiasm' and the fear that evangelical Arminianism would undermine sound doctrine. In England the evangelical Calvinists were led by the Countess of Huntingdon (1707-91) and George Whitefield (1714-70); their American counterpart was Jonathan Edwards (1703-58).

The first indigenous church in Wales resulted from the revival in its Calvinistic form: the Presbyterian (or Calvinistic Methodist) Church of Wales. At first societies were established under such leaders as Howel Harris, Daniel Rowland and Howell Davies — the first dating from 1735; the Church's Confession of Faith and Constitution were adopted in 1832. Revival in Britain and America led to world mission.

In the first half of the nineteenth century the London Missionary Society (1795) established churches in South Africa (1799), Guyana (1808), Mauritius (1814) and Samoa (1836). American missionaries did likewise in Greece (1828), Iran (1834), Chile (1845), Equatorial Guinea (1850). The work of the Basel and Scottish missions bore churchly fruit in Ghana (1828), as did that of the Bremen Mission (1847). Churches were established in Lesotho (1833) under the Paris Mission, and in Northeast India (1841) by the Welsh Presbyterian mission.

From 1850-1900 American missionary efforts resulted in churches in Cameroon (1857) — and the Basel Mission also began work in that country in 1886; Egypt (1854); Brazil (1859); Guatemala (1882); Korea (1885); Zaire (1891). Canadian missionaries were active in Trinidad (1868); Swiss in Mozambique (1887); Dutch in Karo Batak (1890); Scottish in Kenya (1891); while in Rwanda the present Presbyterian Church looks back to the work of the German Bethel Mission, and to that of Belgian, British, Danish and Swiss missionaries.

In the twentieth century churches were established by American missionaries in Cuba (1900), and by Hungarians in Brazil (1932). From Brazil missionaries came to Portugal in 1942 to reawaken the Reformed cause there. The Dutch Reformed Church of South

Africa and (from 1961) the Netherlands Reformed Church are the progenitors of the Reformed Church of East Africa, Kenya (1944).

The above list is by no means exhaustive, but it does indicate the date of formation, and originating mission, of a number of member churches of the World Alliance of Reformed Churches.

4. *Churches resulting from secession.* Alliance members in this category include the Remonstrant Brotherhood (so named from a remonstrance presented in 1610 to the States of Holland in which five articles concerning election were adumbrated; these were countered by the Synod of Dord (1618-19); the Associate Reformed Presbyterian Church (USA) (1782); the Second Cumberland Presbyterian Church (USA) (1874); the Reformed Churches in the Netherlands (1892); the United Free Church of Scotland (1900/1929); the Independent Presbyterian Church of Brazil (1903).

5. *Nineteenth-century evangelical revivals.* In the second half of the nineteenth century revivals occurred in various parts of Europe. From these emerged the Church of the Brethren in Czechoslovakia (1868) and the Swedish Mission Covenant Church (1878). Both are congregational in polity, and the latter has made paedo- and believers' baptism alternatively available from its inception.

6. *Immigrant churches.* These were established by the Dutch in South Africa (1652); the British in Canada (1755), Australia (1830) and New Zealand (1842); by the Scots in Guyana (1815); and by the Hungarians (1921) and Lithuanians in the United States.

7. *United churches.* The Reformed family has witnessed reunions and new unions as well as secessions. Within the family the Church of Scotland united with the majority of the United Free Church in 1929; Congregational and Evangelical and Reformed Christians united to form the United Church of Christ (USA) in 1957; Congregationalists and Presbyterians came together in the United Church of Jamaica and Grand Cayman (1965); and the United Presbyterian Church in the USA united with the (southern) Presbyterian Church in the US to form the Presbyterian Church (U.S.A.) in 1984.

Transconfessional unions include those in Czechoslovakia (Lutheran, Reformed), 1918; Canada (Congregational, Presbyterian, Methodist), 1925; Thailand (Presbyterian, Baptist, Disciples), 1934; the Philippines (Congregational, Presbyterian, Brethren, Methodist, Evangelical), 1948; Zambia (Congregational, Presbyterian, Methodist), 1965; North India (Congregational, Presbyterian,

Anglican, Baptist, Brethren, Disciples, Methodist), 1970; Australia (Congregational, Presbyterian, Methodist), 1977; and the United Kingdom (Congregational, Presbyterian, Churches of Christ), 1981.

The Union Churches of Germany (Lutheran, Reformed) are not in membership of the World Alliance, though they keep contact with it, and the United Church of Christ in Japan is in the same position.

Confessions and Catechisms

Classical Reformed Confessions include the following: Zwingli's Sixty-seven Articles (1523); the First Basel Confession (1534); the First Helvetic Confession (1536); the Geneva Confession (1536); the French Confession (1559); the Scottish Confession (1560); the Belgic Confession (1561); the Second Helvetic Confession (1566); the Westminster Confession (1647). More recent confessions include those of the United Presbyterian Church USA (1967) and the Presbyterian Church in the Republic of Korea (1972). The Presbyterian Church USA is currently preparing a new confession.

Prominent larger catechisms include Calvin's (1541); the Heidelberg (1563); Craig's (1581); the New (1644); and the Larger (1648). Among shorter catechisms are the Little (1556); Craig's (1592); that for Young Children (1641); the Shorter (1648).

Congregational declarations and statements of faith include the following: Browne's Statement of Congregational Principles (1582); the First Confession (1589) and the Second Confession (1596) of the London-Amsterdam Church; the Cambridge Synod and Platform (1646-8); the Savoy Declaration of Faith and Order (1658); the English Congregational Union Declaration (1833); the 'Burial Hill' Declaration (1865); the Constitution of the National Council and the Oberlin Declaration (1871); the 'Commission' Creed (1883); the Declaration of Faith of the Congregational Church in England and Wales (1967).

Whilst neither Presbyterians nor Congregationalists have been reluctant to declare the faith commonly held among them, the former have normally required confessional subscription of at least ministers and elders, the latter have not. Moreover Congregationalists have in their local church covenants experienced corporate confessing at its most intimate.

Polity

Presbyterians and Congregationalists emphasize the corporate priesthood of all believers, and maintain the doctrine of the parity of ministers. Presbyterian and Reformed churches are synodically governed, Congregational churches are locally autonomous. At worst this autonomy has been construed in an isolationist way, but normally inter-dependency has been the rule, and it has been held that the company of gathered saints is the *catholic* church manifest. American Congregationalism was traditionally more synodical than British.

Reformed churches are served by ministers and elders at least; some also maintain a diaconate, and a few the office of doctor (i.e. theological teacher). Some Reformed churches are episcopal, though the office of bishop is not sacerdotally construed. Congregationalists have ministers and deacons, the latter normally having pastoral and spiritual functions akin to those of the Presbyterian elder. The Congregational Church Meeting is the gathering of the Church under Christ to seek his will regarding witness and mission. It is often closely related in time and thought to the sacrament of the Lord's Supper. Here the Saints, nourished by the bread and wine, seek God's mind concerning their ministry and service.

Theology
The confessions and catechisms constitute collections of teaching drawn up by or for, and given within, Reformed churches, and to that extent they may be taken as exemplifying Reformed doctrine. On the other hand, there is no such thing as Reformed doctrine in the sense of a certain number of teachings which are *exclusive* to the Reformed. Neither the Reformers nor the Puritans set out to devise a Reformed theology in the latter sense. Rather, their intentions were catholic, and they sought to provide biblically-based teaching. Moreover, those who produced the confessions and catechisms did not regard their own work as sacrosanct.

There are, however, certain emphases which are characteristic of Reformed teaching: the priority of the free grace of God, who is sovereign Lord of church and world; the maintenance of the Creator-creature distinction; the desire to claim the whole world for God; the concept of the people of God as covenanted to the Lord and to each other.

Reformed scholars have made distinguished contributions in many fields of theological learning, but the following list of those whose work was or is primarily theological will indicate something of the intellectual strength and variety of the tradition: Calvin (1509-64); William Ames (1576-1633); John Owen (1616-83); Francis Turretin (1623-87); Jonathan Edwards (1703-58); F. D. E. Schleiermacher (1768-1834); Charles Hodge (1797-1878); John McLeod Campbell (1800-72); Abraham Kuyper (1837-1920); Andrew Martin Fairbairn (1838-1912); Peter Taylor Forsyth (1848-1921); James Denney (1856-1917); Karl Barth (1886-1968); Reinhold Niebuhr (1892-1971); Thomas Forsyth Torrance (1913-   ).

Worship

Worship in the Reformed family is in many styles. The range is from services in which the unaccompanied singing of metrical psalms only is permitted, to services with choirs and clapping, bands and dancing. The proclamation of the gospel is, however, central, and the dominical sacraments are observed.

In circles penetrated by the modern liturgical movement there have been moves to relate Word and Sacrament more closely together; to express the dialogic nature of worship through the shape of the liturgy; and to utilize the liturgical resources of the ages. Directories of worship rather than formally required liturgies are the norm, and there is a long tradition of these including Calvin's (1540, 1542, 1545), Knox's (1556), A Lasco's (1550, 1555), the Dutch (1566), and the Westminster (1644).

Guidance is not always, and sometimes not at all, followed — yet freedom within order is the goal. An important place is given to conceived and extempore prayer.

Reformed hymn writers are legion, but among them Isaac Watts (1674-1748) and Philip Doddridge (1702-51) reign supreme. A notable succession of distinguished (and sometimes idiosyncratic and autocratic) preachers includes Joseph Parker (1830-1902) and Alexander Whyte (1836-1921).

Liturgical ideas (or the lack of them) have influenced church architecture, which ranges from the early meetinghouse style which permits the people to gather around pulpit and table; through the period of 'aping the Anglicans' with cruciform buildings, and of undue operatic influence which led to galleried auditoria in which the choir had lofty prominence (on the quaint assumption that it was there to *perform)* and the 'bandstand' pulpit dwarfed the communion table; to the open plan arrangements of today.

International Bodies

1. *The World Alliance of Reformed Churches (1875/1891/1970).* As we have seen, this body unites two confessional families whose world bodies were founded for fellowship and mutual support, and neither of which had executive powers; and it includes some sixteen united churches.

The idea of holding a regular Presbyterian International Council was first proposed in the 1860's by James MacGregor, James McCosh and others. William Garden Blaikie, another distinguished pioneer, became the first president (1888-92). In 1874, Hastings Ross published an article on 'an ecumenical council of Congregational churches', and Henry Martyn Dexter and Alexander Hannay were among early advocates of such an idea. The Presbyterian Alliance held 19 Councils prior to the union of 1970; the International Congregational Council held 10. A Centennial Consultation in 1977 was followed by the twenty-second Council at Ottawa (1982).

The Alliance is based in Geneva and has three departments. The General Secretariat is concerned with over-all policy, membership, public relations and finance. The Department of Theology (1959) facilitates theological sharing among member churches; engages in dialogue with other Christian world communions (dialogues with Anglicans and Baptists are completed; conversations with Mennonites and Roman Catholics are in progress; and talks with Methodists, Lutherans, Disciples, and with the Orthodox Churches are planned); maintains contact with 290 Reformed-related theological faculties and colleges; runs a scholarship scheme; and conducts a program of research into the thought, history, and present significance of the Reformed tradition. The Department of Cooperation and Witness (1965) is concerned with the Alliance's publications, with news and information, and with questions of human rights, religious and civil liberties, and peace and justice — especially as these pertain to member churches of the Alliance.

Current Alliance-wide concerns include the Covenant for Peace and Justice, devised by the Executive Committee in 1983, and now commended to other Christian world communions as something in which they may care to join; and a special study program based upon the booklet, *Called to Witness to the Gospel Today*. This challenges member churches to ask themselves what it means to confess Christ today in their several contexts, and invites them to share their findings with a view to a global testimony to be made at the next General Council (1989).

The Alliance has a European Committee and a Caribbean and North American Area Council (which also has its Theological Committee). These meet regularly and share in the total program of the Alliance.

A General Council is held every 5-7 years, and the Executive Committee of 32 members meets normally every year.

The Alliance maintains contact with the two bodies to be mentioned below, and also with the World Council of Churches and the other Christian world communions.

Membership of the Alliance is difficult to compute because some churches count all the baptized, others only the professed believers. However, a conservative estimate of 50-60 millions may be made.

2. *The Reformed Ecumenical Synod (1946).* Based in Grand Rapids, USA, this body unites more than thirty Reformed and Presbyterian churches of a traditionally confessional kind. Total membership is between 5 and 6 millions. About one third of RES member churches also belong to WARC.

3. *The International Congregational Fellowship (1977).* Unlike the other two bodies, this is a voluntary association of *individuals* who meet for fellowship, and in order to witness to Congregational insights concerning church polity and freedom under the gospel. Some members belong to unions which are members of WARC, others do not.

A number of Presbyterian and Congregational churches are not in formal contact with any of the above bodies. The World Alliance endeavors to keep in touch with some of them.

Bibliography

Arthur C. Cochrane (ed.), *Reformed Confession of the 16th Century* (1966); T. F. Torrance (ed.), *The School of Faith: The Catechisms of the Reformed Church* (1959); L. Vischer (ed.), *Reformed Witness Today* (1982); Williston Walker, *The Creeds and Platforms of Congregationalism* (1960); G. G. Atkins and F. L. Fagley, *History of American Congregationalism* (1942); Tudur Jones, *Congregationalism in England* (1962); T. M. Lindsay, *History of the Reformation,* 2 vols. (1907); J. T. McNeill, *The History and Character of Calvinism* (1954); G. F. Nuttall, *Visible Saints: The Congregational Way, 1640-1660* (1957); Daniel Jenkins, *Congregationalism: A Restatement* (1954); Alan Sell, *Saints: Visible, Orderly and Catholic: The Congregational Idea of the Church* (forthcoming); John Leith, *Introduction to the Reformed Tradition* (1981); John M. Barclay, *The Worship of the Reformed Church* (1966); Horton Davies, *The Worship of the English Puritans* (1948); Bryan D. Spinks, *Freedom or Order? The Eucharistic Liturgy in English Congregationalism, 1645-1980* (1984); Ralph Calder (ed.) *To Introduce the Family* (1953); Albert Peel and Douglas Horton, *International Congregationalism* (1949); Marcel Pradervand, *A Century of Service, A History of the World Alliance of Reformed Churches, 1875-1975* (1975); *Handbook of (WARC) Member Churches* (1982); *Proceedings* of the World Presbyterian Alliance and of the International Congregational Council; *Acts* of the Reformed Ecumenical Synod; *Reports* of the International Congregational Fellowship.

NOTE: The above article will appear in German in *Oekumene-Lexikon,* Frankfurt: Verlag Otto Lembeck, 2nd edn., 1986. It is used here by kind permission of the Editor, Dr. Walter Muller-Romheld.

For an investigation of the relations between the Congregational wing of the Reformed family and the Anabaptists/Mennonites see Alan P.F. Sell, 'Anabaptist-Congregational relations and current Mennonite-Reformed dialogue', *The Mennonite Quarterly Review,* forthcoming.

Who are the Reformed Today?

JEAN-MARC CHAPPUIS

The First Question

Are the Reformed churches today what they were in the 16th century when they emerged from medieval Christianity, propelled by the reform movement which at that time gripped the entire Church at its very roots? The appropriate answer is both Yes and No.

1. *Answering Yes.* Continuity across four intervening centuries is obvious if we consider the two principles which gave the Reformed churches their specific identity: *sola scriptura:* Scripture alone is the rule, the canon, the norm of revelation; and *sola gratia:* God's grace in Christ and through the Spirit is the only source of salvation.

For all the doctrinal variations of Reformed Protestantism, evident to the observer, whatever his historical or geographical vantage point, the permanence of these two original principles is clearly visible in filigree. These two principles, shining through all the variations, give the Reformed churches their specific unity and fundamental identity in the contemporary ecumenical dialogue.

The Reformed churches, as they have always done, are asking how they are to be faithful to their fundamental principles today. In *Called to Witness to the Gospel Today* (1982), the World Alliance of Reformed churches puts to member churches two questions concerning the authority of Scripture.

Question one relates to the nature of this authority: 'How are we to restate the Reformers' views of Scripture consistently with what we know of the Bible's complex history of development?'

Question two concerns the relation between the authority of Scripture and the work of the Holy Spirit: 'The Spirit which inspired the authors of Scripture is at work in the church today. How is this interrelation best expressed?'

In respect of free salvation too, the Alliance considers the question of the relation of faith to works: 'How should the Church attend to a rightful "disciple-ing" of the people of God at every level of the Christian life?' The fact is that 'the danger of legalism' is no valid ground for not recognizing that 'from the doctrinal point of view, justification and sanctification in an ordered common life go together'.

These are legitimate questions which every generation must face anew and take responsibility for the answers they prompt. These questions in no way cast doubt on the two original principles of the Reformed churches. Quite the reverse. They bear witness to the vitality and practical value of these principles in a Reformed church which knows itself to be always in need of reformation, *semper reformanda*.

Yes, the Reformed churches today are indeed what they were in the 16th century! The two greatest theological personalities of the Reformed churches, John Calvin in the age of Reformation and Karl Barth in the 20th century, both displayed the same firmness and inflexibility in insisting on the pertinence of the *sola scriptura* for the doctrine of revelation and of the *sola gratia* for the doctrine of salvation. Such, then, is the Yes that we must utter in answer to our question.

2. *Answering No.* What of the No that we must also utter today in response to this question? I shall define this No in terms of the comparison just made between Calvin and Barth and in terms of their respective ecclesiologies, which typify their two different epochs. Calvin and Barth are, in fact, not only the two outstanding theological figures of the Reformed churches, but also representative in the highest degree of their respective times. They were not only thinkers, but also activists, fully engaged in the struggles which the Gospel constrained them to wage in human society. The circumstances and distinguishing features of these struggles are not identical. The battlefront has shifted.

Living within a 'Christian' system, Calvin sought the reform of the Western church. The central question for him is where the true Church is to be found. The answer he offers, following in the steps of Luther, consists in the marks of the true church, the faithful preaching of the Gospel and the administration of the sacraments in accordance with Christ's will, marks which he considered to be scripturally irrefutable.

Locked in combat with the anti-semitic and racist neo-paganism of the Nazi regime, Barth attacks religion, understood as sinful humanity's annexation of the divine. His central question is: where is the church? Now the Church is not necessarily in the institution which is supposed to represent it, since faith in Jesus Christ is found in that institution in a form perverted by paganism. The Church exists where two or three are gathered together in the name of Jesus Christ, confessing their faith uncompromisingly and witnessing to Christ's lordship over the world.

The difference between the Reformed Christians of the 16th century and those of the 20th century will therefore emerge in respect of the Church and of the conception it has of itself.

In his 'Doctrine of Reconciliation'[1] in a paragraph entitled 'The Holy Spirit and the Sending of the Christian Community', Barth identifies a 'gap' in the Reformed, as well as in the Patristic and Scholastic doctrine of the church. This gap consists in the flagrant absence of any clear perception of the goal which the Church was meant to serve.

'It is plain that in the depictions of the 16th and 17th centuries we do not find any goal of its existence transcending the Church itself, its ordered activity and the temporal and eternal life of its members. According to Calvin ... its only function is to be, as Cyprian puts it, the mother of believers as God is their Father...' [2]

This astonishes Barth:

'It is rather strange that Calvin's meritorious and significant rediscovery of the prophetic office of Jesus Christ did not work itself out either in his own doctrine of the Church or in that of his followers. *"He was the sovereign messenger and ambassador of God His Father, to give a full exposition of God's will toward the world"* — is what Calvin wrote in this connection in the *Geneva Catechism*. How far does this *toward the world* extend in practice? Has not the work of this divine messenger and ambassador actually ceased in the blind alley of the Church as an institution of salvation for those who belong to it?' [3]

This radically critical question addressed by Barth to Calvin clearly reveals how the Reformed churches' conception of their ecclesial character has evolved in the intervening 400 years. It is permissible to ask, however, whether Barth's criticism is really justified. If we take account only of Book 4 of the *Institutio,* devoted to 'the External Means or Aids by which God invites us into the Society of Christ and holds us therein', we might be tempted to imagine that in Calvin the church's role is reduced to a purely instrumental one, that of mother to believers. An alert reading of the entire work, however, will not permit us to rest there. We soon realize that the Church is not only the instrument of the calling and sanctification of believers, but also itself, as a community, an object of faith. Alexandre Ganoczy, one of the finest of Catholic Calvin scholars, saw and stated this clearly:

'We certainly have to recognize that the first decisive document of the Catholic magisterium to expound the nature of the Church in terms of the scriptural concept of the Body of Christ, i.e. the Encyclical *Mystici corporis,* dates only from 1943, whereas Calvin had already constructed his entire ecclesiology on this basis as long ago as 1536'. [4]

It would also seem unwarranted to say that Christ's prophetic work 'did not work itself out... but actually ceased in the church' under the Calvinist regime. For the corporative church, as Calvin understood it, gave birth to a genuine community personalism whose historical influence and effects in the life of societies, in politics, in law, and in the question of civil liberties, are manifest. By liberating Christians from the traditional clerical and hierarchical ascendancy, Calvinism equipped them to envisage new forms of common life. One has only to recall here the 'covenant' made by the Pilgrim Fathers of New England aboard the *Mayflower* in 1620, or of the constitution of Rhode Island in 1663, the work of Roger Williams. The doctrine of the inner witness of the Holy Spirit bore manifest fruits in the concept of freedom of conscience which finds expression here.

Barth's criticism of Calvin's ecclesiology seems hardly warranted, therefore. On the other hand, what strikes us positively here is the original ecclesiological conception which Barth develops on the basis of this criticism. Fortified by his dramatic personal encounter with the return of paganism to Europe in full force, Barth gives a new dimension to the church's conception of itself by setting it within a perspective wholly dominated by eschatology and mission, something which would have been quite inconceivable for the reformers of western Christendom in the 16th century.

The Christian community has a goal which transcends the salvation of its members: it is a 'community for the world'. On this understanding, moreover, it is only gathered, upbuilt and sent through the power of the Holy Spirit; it is 'the provisional representation *(vorläufige Darstellung)* of humanity as a whole' which God calls, justifies and sanctifies. The words used here bear a considerable force. The Church is a 'provisional representation' of the salvation of humanity as a whole. The Church, in fact, is not part of the order of creation. In this world it has no place of its own, and, in particular, no 'religious' place which is a constant dimension of the condition of sinful humanity. It is 'provisional' because it manifests, as a precursory sign, the coming Kingdom of God. It is part of the order of reconciliation. It is an eschatological magnitude.

It is also the 'provisional representation' of the salvation of 'humanity as a whole'. It is a 'community for the world' because it does not exist for itself but to witness that salvation is offered to all. It is wholly and completely mission.

This far too cursory summary of Barth's ecclesiology reveals at one and the same time the distance travelled since the 16th century, and the way in which the Church's idea of itself has meanwhile been transformed in Reformed theology. The Church, an eschatological magnitude, is wholly and completely mission! No one who knows the field will deny that these two basic characteristics of the church were *not* clearly articulated in the 16th century: not by Calvin, nor by Luther or Zwingli, who, on the contrary, completely ignored them. But they were clearly articulated by people of various allegiances known as the 'Anabaptists', a quite inadequate generic term, or nearer the mark, as the 'Radicals'. Nor is it any accident that Barth, who rediscovers and adopts two of their basic intuitions, should at the same time call in question the infant baptism so vigorously commended by Calvin and rejected equally vigorously by the Radicals! For everything here is interconnected and coherent when a fresh mind is brought to bear on the clarification of the church's situation in the contemporary world in the light of Scripture.

This comparison, confined to two outstanding theological figures such as Calvin and Barth, retains its significance when the horizon is widened beyond their individual persons and works. Not everyone in the Reformed Churches is a 'Barthian', far from it. But for at least a century now, the awareness of the church as a missionary community has become the rule among Reformed Christians. As for eschatology, this too has recovered its place in such different currents of thought as that of Albert Schweitzer yesterday and that of Jürgen Moltmann today.

This being so, a dialogue in depth between 'Reformed' and 'Radicals', and in particular between Reformed and Mennonites, once again becomes possible. Certainly their overall outlooks are different. The former are the descendants of those who set out to reform the Western church. The latter are the heirs of those who took the re-establishment of the primitive church as their objective. Merciless struggles were waged between them at that time, even though at Strasbourg or in Hesse, for example, efforts were made to make these two related, yet divergent, movements mutually enriching.

The Central Issue

Today the dialogue between Reformed and Radicals is possible at a deep level. The merciless struggles of those former times are a thing of the past. While the overall outlooks on either side may remain different, it could be that they will increasingly be seen to be complementary, and no longer as a sterile antagonism. But we must concentrate more on the central issue at stake.

In his preface to Neal Blough's fine book *Christologie anabaptiste,* Marc Lienhard suggests that the central question is, in the final analysis, not that of baptism itself, but the following:

'The essential thing, it seems to me, is the Anabaptist challenge as to the place of the Church in society. It is the search for a Church which is different from society as a whole, a Church which in its message and its life, expresses the otherness of the Gospel and of the Christian life.'[5]

If we accept that this is the central question, then a first comment springs immediately to mind. Anticipating in the 16th century an evolution whose coming they longed to see and strove to hasten, the Radicals thought of the Christian community as independent of the State and distinct from civil society. Working and reflecting in terms of a 'Christian' system, Luther, Zwingli and Calvin, like their 'Papist' adversaries, did not take this way. The later Pietist movement, and Zinzendorf in particular, and then the 'Awakening' of the 19th century, and Alexandre Vinet in particular, challenged this homogeneity between the Christian community and the civil community. The stimulus provided by these currents certainly helped considerably to modify the Reformed churches' conception of themselves and their relationship to civil society and the State.

Today, however, it is obvious that many of the Reformed churches throughout the world are in the situation of a minority. This is certainly as true in the United States of America, in a constitutional regime based on the separation of Church and State which would have been inconceivable for original Calvinism, as in Algeria in a Muslim society. It is also true in black Africa, in Asia and in Latin America. It is also true in many countries of Europe, both East and West, in Poland as in Portugal.

This situation, the daily experience to which it gives rise and the ecclesial practice typical of it, give most of the Reformed churches a self-awareness which obviously no longer has much in common with the outlook of the Christendom against which the Radicals of the 16th century struggled! The sharing of the lessons learned in such conditions is certainly one of the most promising pathways of dialogue in depth which our epoch opens up in future between Reformed and Radicals.

At the theological level, however, the point to be recognized is that the capacity to reinterpret itself in this direction already existed potentially in Calvinism from the beginning; not only because in John Calvin's own country the Reformed churches remained in a minority, but also because Calvin himself viewed the question of the church's place in society differently from Luther and Zwingli, his predecessors of the first generation of reformers.

In respect of the subject which concerns us here, Calvin appears in a somewhat paradoxical light. In his major work, *The Anabaptist View of the Church,* Franklin Hamlin Littell has this to say of Calvin: 'Of all the many authors I have read, none probably understood the Anabaptists less!' [6] This comment is not without a certain touch of humor when it is remembered that Idelette de Bure, the Reformer's wife, came from an Anabaptist background, being the widow of an Anabaptist whom Calvin had convinced of his error! But what Littell undoubtedly means is that Calvin did not find himself confronted directly with the Anabaptists in Geneva as did Luther in Wittenberg and Zwingli in Zurich. Calvinist Geneva certainly burnt a 'rationalist' named Michel Servetus, but it did not throw Anabaptists into the river as they were indeed thrown into the Limmat...

Calvin, then, did not understand the Anabaptists; indeed, according to Littell, he confused them with the individualistic medieval spiritualists and mystics. On the other hand, he at once saw the need in Geneva to differentiate between the Christian community and the civil community, between Church and State. In this episcopal princedom from which the prince-bishop had fled and in which Calvin arrived on the morrow of the promulgation of the reform edicts in 1536, the French Reformer would display an unshakeable firmness in insisting on a distribution of powers respecting the independence of the church. Geneva became a Republic. Naturally, therefore, it was to the magistrate that the temporal power of the prince-bishop reverted. But there was no question of the magistrate's inheriting or assuming the spiritual power of the prince-bishop. But Geneva no longer had a bishop? That need be no obstacle! Calvin rightly and very effectively turned his attention to the institutional question (with all due respect to Karl Barth!), to what at that time was called 'the order of the Church'. A lawyer by training, a pastor and an exceptional theologian, Calvin would endow the Church of Geneva with specific independent instruments, making it impossible for the magistrate to usurp episcopal powers. Doctrinal authority would be invested in the Company of Pastors, a collegial body, while disciplinary powers would be assigned to the Consistory, also a collegial body. This characteristically Calvinist structure marked Reformed Geneva off very clearly at that time from the other Reformed Swiss cantons as well as from the German princedoms which had become Lutheran.

In a collective work entitled *L'Eglise et l'Etat, évolution de leurs rapports,* Johannes Georg Fuchs points out that it took three centuries for the Reformed Churches of Switzerland to acquire (at long last!) specific institutional organs:

> 'It was only in the latter half of the 19th century that we find the Evangelical Reformed Churches providing themselves with institutional organs of their own. ... It was under the constitution of 1874 that the decisive step was taken in this direction.' [7]

What was already the case in Geneva since 1542, thus became the case for the other Reformed churches of the Swiss cantons only in 1874. Our purpose in underlining this point here is for the light this difference throws on the capacity inherent in Calvinism from the very beginning to reinterpret itself on the basis of a clear distinction between Christian community and civil community, between Church and State.

Nor was it any accident that the people of Geneva should in 1907 have voted for the suppression of the church budget. From that time forth, as later in Neuchâtel, but in contrast to the other Reformed Swiss cantons, the Reformed Church of Geneva no longer benefited from State subsidies or from an obligatory church tax.

The fact is that this suppression, typical of modern times, was already present in embryo in the distribution of the powers of the prince-bishop which took place in Geneva in the 16th century.

Yet this church still bears the name — the *National* Protestant Church of Geneva! It is quite clear from this that the overall outlook of the Reformed still differs from that of the Radicals, although there has been a radical reinterpretation of the eschatological dimension of the Church, of the missionary mandate which has been entrusted to it until the end of time, and of the place of the church in society, by the Reformed themselves in the direction of a convergence of all these dimensions.

The reason for this retention of the label 'National' in its name is, doubtless, because the Reformed churches, especially in countries where Christianity first gained a foothold in the early centuries and even more so in countries where they are in a majority, are keenly aware of their inescapable responsibility to offer the opportunity of hearing and accepting the Gospel to *all,* to the rising generation, to the sick in the hospitals, to those serving in the military forces, to television audiences, to the magistrates who direct civic affairs. Their being 'multitudinaries', churches for the whole people, handicaps them somewhat, so that they are unable alone always to offer to our contemporaries the profile of a pioneering unit called by God to be the 'provisional representation' of the salvation of humanity as a whole. The Radicals have other assets which make their witness indispensable for the full performance of the mission which the Risen Christ entrusted to the apostles and disciples of the infant church.

'Community for the world' — only as it is faithful to the Word of God as attested in Holy Scripture can the Church of Jesus Christ be this 'community for the world'. Yet it is unquestionably in diversity that it must be this community, for while Scripture knows of only one Gospel, it required four evangelists to present this unique Gospel to us!

FOOTNOTES:

[1] Karl Barth, *Church Dogmatics,* Edinburgh: T. & T. Clark, 1962.

[2] Ibid., p. 766.

[3] Ibid., p. 766f.

[4] Alexandre Ganoczy, *Calvin, théologien de l'Eglise et du ministère,* Paris: Cerf, 1964, p. 420.

[5] Neal Blough, *Christologie anabaptiste,* Geneva: Labor et Fides, 1984, p. 11.

[6] F.H. Littell, *The Anabaptist View of the Church,* Beacon Hill, Boston: Star King Press.

[7] Johannes Georg Fuchs et al. *L'Eglise et l'Etat, évolution de leurs rapports,* Berne 1974, p. 35.

Extract from the oldest manuscript of the "Articles of Schleitheim" (February 24, 1527); possibly written by Michael Sattler (†May 21, 1527). (Municipal Archives of Bern).

The Attitude of the Reformed Churches Today to the Condemnations of the Baptists in the Reformed Confessional Documents *

The Problem

'*We condemn the Anabaptists, who deny that newborn infants of the faithful are to be baptized. For according to evangelical teaching, of such is the Kingdom of God, and they are in the covenant of God. Why, then, should the sign of God's covenant not be given to them?*'

'*We condemn the Anabaptists, who, when they deny that a Christian may hold the office of a magistrate, deny also that a man may be justly put to death by the magistrate, or that the magistrate may wage war, or that oaths are to be rendered to a magistrate, and such like things.*'

These statements are found in the *Second Helvetic Confession* (chs. 20 and 30). Regarded as one of the classic summaries of Reformed doctrine, this confession continues to be held in high regard by many churches. How do the Reformed churches stand today in respect to these repudiations? Are these denials still valid? Or have we arrived at a different attitude to the tradition of which Mennonites are the heirs?

To begin with, one point is clear: to the extent that these repudiations were used to justify the oppression and persecution of the Anabaptists, the Reformed churches must dissociate themselves from them. Repudiation of their teaching should not in any case have been permitted to end in public prosecutions, executions and banishments. The Reformed churches have no right to ignore the wrongs done to the Anabaptists in the course of the centuries or even to use any arguments whatever to excuse these wrongs. They must frankly admit this somber and shameful aspect of their history. Reformed Christians have themselves often been among the persecuted; they are not entitled to forget that they were sometimes also to be found in the ranks of the persecutors.

---

* The final version of this article has been formulated by the Reformed members of the team of editors; they bear responsibility especially for the conclusions. The historical material has been prepared by *Professor Dr. Ernst Saxer* (Bern). The editors wish to express their deep gratitude for his careful research work.

This thought was clearly expressed by a representative of the Reformed Church at a united communion service in the Grossmünster in Zurich on March 5, 1983:

'We thank You for all that Your Spirit has accomplished in Your Church throughout the centuries since the first ages. We thank Your for all who have witnessed to the Gospel by their words and by their lives. We thank You especially for the Reformers to whose work and witness Your Church owes so much.

In Your presence we also confess, however, how often we have shut our ears to the voice of Your Spirit, preferring our own ideas and discoveries. In Your presence and in the presence of our Mennonite sisters and brothers, we confess today how often we Reformed Christians failed to understand what You wanted to say to Your Church through the witness and work of our fellow Christians in the Free Churches. We remember before You the wrongs that were done to them in our own country throughout the years: persecution, oppression, execution, banishment.

Lord our God, show us now Your grace and mercy. Forgive us and help us to begin afresh together today through the power of reconciliation and love, so that the wounds may be healed and fellowship between us grow and deepen. Lord, have mercy upon us.'

The Reformed churches ask forgiveness for the suffering which they brought upon a community which had to obey its own conscience. But how do we deal with the repudiations written into our Reformed confessions of faith? This is a question which is still unanswered in the 1983 Grossmünster prayer.

It is possible simply to ignore these statements. We can explain that they refer to ancient quarrels which no longer concern us. But is that good enough? Are we not required, rather, to say what we think of these things today? Can we look our Mennonite fellow Christians in the face without such an explicit answer to this question? Surely not! Even if it is the case that we no longer go along with them, these statements are still on the record; it would be a mistake to imagine that they no longer exercised any influence on the Reformed churches. Their very place in the confessions also secures them a firm place in the Reformed tradition.

Do we have to say forthrightly that our 16th and 17th century forerunners were simply mistaken in their judgement? Or do we perhaps still have to recognize an element of truth in these statements even today? A clear answer to these questions is essential if the dialogue between our two traditions is to be fruitful and fellowship between us is to grow.

But first let us look at a brief survey of the most important affirmations of the Reformed confessional documents.

I. HISTORICAL SURVEY

1. *Zwingli's Fidei ratio (1530).* The first confessional document which contains Anabaptist condemnations is Ulrich Zwingli's *Fidei ratio.* Strictly speaking, this document cannot be called a confession. It had been written by Zwingli as a private paper for the Augsburg Reichstag of 1530. In this work, however, Zwingli felt himself to be speaking on behalf of the churches influenced by his reform movement.

The struggles against the Anabaptists had begun much earlier. It had been going on both in Zurich and in the whole of the imperial territory since 1525, with council decrees, mandates, condemnations and executions. With the Augsburg Reichstag looming up on the horizon, therefore, a clear dissociation from the Anabaptists was undoubtedly in the interests of the Reformation churches. No one who wanted to be recognized by the current imperial law could possibly have anything to do with the Anabaptists. Zwingli repudiated the Anabaptists basically on the ground of their separatism. In the *Fidei ratio,* however, theological considerations take a back seat; Zwingli's main purpose was to demonstrate his accord both with imperial law and with ancient church doctrine. He wrote:

'The Anabaptists are utterly wrong in rejecting the baptism of the children of believers, but not only on this point but also in many other things about which I cannot speak in this place. I have, moreover, trusting in God's help, been the first to teach and write in opposition to them, not without risk, in order to protect our people from their folly and wickedness, so that now, through God's goodness, this sickness has strikingly diminished among our people. That shows how little I accept or defend anything coming from this rebellious party.'

As the quotation shows, Zwingli hardly deals with the peculiar doctrines of the Anabaptists, but is content simply to describe them as a 'rebellious party'. At only one point does he make an exception. He refers explicitly to the doctrine of 'the restoration of all things' as taught by Hans Denck (died in Basel in 1527) and attacks the Anabaptist view that the phrase 'for ever' does not mean a future extending beyond the general judgement. For, Zwingli argues, that would mean there was no Hell for the devil, the mockers of God, and human monsters.

2. *The Synod of Bern (1532).* This confession deserves special mention because it contains no express condemnation of the Anabaptists. The text was composed in 1532 at the request of the Bern City Council by Wolfgang Capito. Influenced by Anabaptist and Schwenkfeldian ideas, by inward conviction Capito stood midway between the emerging fronts. He was impressed by the desire of the Anabaptists to live a Christlike life. He saw common ground in

the conviction that grace achieves its goal 'by an inner course', and on this basis he sought to establish unity between the official Reformed Church and the radical groups. His endeavor accorded with the policy of the Bern government which until 1538 was seeking to win back the Anabaptists by an alternation of negotiations and severe penalties. Only at one place does the Confession mention the Anabaptists:

> In this the poor Anabaptists have been wanting. They set aside external government... and compel and constrain each other, contrary to God's order, 'to abandon house and home, wife and child, father and mother' (Mk. 10:29). It is God's will that we should await His special summons and not undertake anything of ourselves. But above all we should set His love over all things and thereby accept Christ Jesus without external compulsion.

Capito shows understanding for the Anabaptists and even sympathizes with them. By their literalist and legalistic view of Scripture, they are forced to withdraw from the civic life of Christian society. Capito, too, takes the view that Christ's spiritual government is more essential and the secular government to be shown less respect. But even if the Christian 'outgrows the world and the civil authority', he nevertheless remains in the body and therefore still 'subject to the sword and the external administration'.

When the Bern Synod speaks of infant baptism and church excommunication, we find it implicitly dissociating itself from the Anabaptists. Here, too, Capito sticks to this basic argument: it would be wrong to declare certain articles to be decisive and use external force to compel their recognition; to do so would tear church communion asunder; what is required, on the contrary, is persistence in love within the fellowship and the main emphasis should be on inward and spiritual edification.

In the section on the Sacraments (ch. 19), he makes the following general demand: 'Let us try as far as we possibly can to avoid all wrangling and the framing of articles whereby we seek to bind others and bring them to our opinion and enforce this on them.'

As for the excommunication of notorious sinners, this should be left exclusively to the common court.

The Synod has this to say about baptism (ch. 21):

When we are too much concerned with outward things, we are thereby 'hindered in the contemplation of the eternal deeds of God which happened in faith...' We should not let ourselves be burdened with the deviant fancies of excitable people who mean well, certainly, but lead the simple astray to superstition on account of external actions. We take care, therefore, to maintain uniformity in the rites of baptism, and not to say, as some do: 'Being free, I shall baptize as I please. Why should

I worry what others do?' No, dear brothers, not so! Certainly a Christian is free, but he shows consideration for all. His wish is to unsettle none, to scandalize none. We are free, but as servants of justice and 'everyone's servant for Christ's sake'. What kind of Christian love is it, however, when I cannot conform in external things to a whole city or whole country and cannot adapt myself to the same forms? We hope, then, that no one will be so shameless as to accept a special rite.

The Bern Synod constitutes an exception among Reformed confessions in its emphatic refusal to fix in dogmatic terms the difference with the Anabaptists. What it complains of, rather, is their separation from the constituted State Church. On the basis of an extremely pneumatological and internalized view of faith, the confession tries to relativize the external orders of the Church. Although these orders are indispensable, basically they are no more than a reflection of, and a prop for, the saving process taking place inwardly in the action of divine grace. The confession rests content with this attempted relativization. It can no longer annul the division already consummated.

In these first two confessions, the *Fidei ratio* and the *Bern Synod,* the Anabaptists are seen as a group on the point of separating from church communion out of a mistaken striving for holiness.

3. *The Basel Confession (1534) and the Confessio Helvetica prior (1536).* The Basel Confession was composed by Oswald Myconius in 1534. By it the Reformation was finally established and completed in this city on the Rhine. The *Confessio Helvetica prior* (the *First Helvetic Confession)* owed its composition to a specific extraneous circumstance. When Pope Paul III announced the convocation of a general council in Mantua in 1537, the Reformed churches of Switzerland felt it necessary to formulate a common confession of their faith. Heinrich Bullinger, Simon Grynaeus, Oswald Myconius, Kaspar Megander and Leo Jud participated in the drafting of this confession.

Both confessions contain an explicit condemnation of the Anabaptists. In Article 6, the *Basel Confession* attacks the 'errors of the Anabaptists', while the *First Helvetic Confession,* after its treatment of the question of the Sacraments and the Church, devotes a separate article to those who 'divide the Church by false doctrines or else separate from it and form voluntary associations' (art. 24). Zwingli's view continues to be determinative. The Anabaptists are viewed as a rebellious, separatist group. They are described as *'Rottengeister'* (1534) or as people 'who hive off from the holy community and society of the Church' (1536).

The new feature, however, is that both these confessions devote a separate article to the repudiation of the Anabaptists. Another new feature is the doctrinal specification of the condemnation. In the *Basel Confession,* the rejection of infant baptism, the oath and the Christian character of civil government, is explicitly repudiated on the basis of Zwinglian arguments. The probable target aimed at in this condemnation are the Anabaptist Articles of Schleitheim of 1527. The *First Helvetic Confession* goes still further. It refers in general terms to 'the strange ungodly doctrines' to which 'the Anabaptists in particular adhere', and states explicitly that they are to be 'punished and suppressed by the civil magistrate' if they stubbornly persist in their 'false doctrines'. In view of the relevant provisions of imperial law, the authors of the *First Helvetic Confession* evidently thought it necessary to include in their document an explicit reference to the duty of the civil magistrate in the matter of heresy.

As we see, the upshot of the developing situation is that the Reformed and the Anabaptists begin to accustom themselves to separation. Unity is no longer considered possible. The repudiation takes on a fixed confessional form. The *Basel Confession* also speaks for the first time of 'condemned doctrinal views'. Its authors may have been influenced by the *Confessio Augustana* which includes a series of repudiations of the Anabaptists (Articles 9, 16, 17).

4. *The Frankfurt Confession (1554).* This Confession was composed by the Dutch refugee community on its return from England. The community had to defend itself against the charge of Anabaptist leanings. The confession ends with the following brief declaration: 'We solemnly abjure all associations, falsely called churches, such as the Mohammedans, Anabaptists, Libertinists, Mennonites, Marcionites, Arians, etc.'

The first point to strike us here is that Mennonites are mentioned as a separate group alongside the Anabaptists. Also noteworthy is the fact that the Anabaptists appear here for the first time in a list which includes Mohammedans and the heretics of the ancient Church. In the *Confessio Helvetica posterior* (the Second Helvetic Confession) this feature will be still more clearly profiled.

5. *Confessions strongly influenced by Calvin: Confession de Foy (1559), Confessio Scotica (1560), Confessio Belgica (1561).* The Anabaptists are not explicitly mentioned in the *Confession of Reformed France* (1559). But various statements clearly have them in mind.

Article 25 explicitly condemns 'all utopians *("fantastiques")* who... would like to abolish the ministry and preaching of the Word of God and the sacraments'. It is not impossible that the example of the *Confessio Augustana* (art. 5 on the office of the 'ministry') has had some influence. But fundamental here is certainly Calvin's defence of the church's ministry. In *Institutio* of 1539 he deals with the Anabaptists in this connection; he speaks of Satan who 'now with the same malice... is striving to overthrow the ministry, a ministry Christ so ordained in the church that, if destroyed, the upbuilding of the church would fail' (*Inst.* IV. 1.11). Article 28 deals with a 'second baptism' which is described as unnecessary. Even as administered in the papal church, baptism is valid and, despite the corruption which prevails there, has retained its essence. This section, in our view, is not concerned with the Anabaptists but seeks to answer the question as to whether baptized children are to be rebaptized by the Reformed Church. It is the ancient church question of heretical baptism which is dealt with here.

It is a different matter in Article 35. Appealing to Mt. 19:14 and I Cor. 7:14, the final statement insists that 'by the authority of Jesus Christ, the infant children of believers are to be baptized'. Infant baptism is defended here not theologically on the basis of broad argumentation but simply with the biblical reference that 'God receives the little children with their parents into His Church.'

Earlier, in Article 11, the question of original sin is dealt with; it had been stated there that 'even after baptism there continues to be sin, in the sense of guilt, even if among the children of God the condemnation has been removed... (Rom. 7). (Original sin) ... is a perversity which still produces fruits of malice and rebellion, so that even the saintliest, though they still resist, never cease to be stained with infirmities and faults as long as they dwell in this world.' While the text does not refer explicitly to the Anabaptists it does make use of a polemical argument from Calvin's *Institutio* which is there directed expressly against the Anabaptists. Although the Anabaptists are not directly mentioned in the Confession, the criticism is in substance even sharper here than in Calvin.

Finally, Article 40 contains a formal condemnation of those 'who would reject the higher authorities *("supériorités")*, establish community of property, and overthrow the order of justice'. The model for this repudiation is a corresponding section in Calvin's 'Short instruction... against the errors... of the Anabaptists' (1544), the Geneva Reformer's pamphlet against the French version of the Schleitheim Articles.

The Anabaptists are mentioned only once in the *Confessio Scotica*. In Chapter 23, 'To quhome Sacramentis appertene', the error of the Anabaptists 'quho denye Baptisme to apperteine to Childrene before that they have faith and understanding' is condemned. As elsewhere in the *Confessio Scotica,* Zwinglian ideas are influential here. In the *Fidei ratio,* Zwingli had still indeed taken the view that, as sign of incorporation into the Church, baptism presupposed either the confession of faith or the reference to the covenant of God.

Chapter 24 deals with the 'Civile Magistrat', declaring that 'sic as resiste the supreme power (doing that thing quhilk appertenis to his charge) do resiste godis ordinance (Roma. 13:2) and thairfore can not be giltless'. To maintain true religion is also part of the State's responsibility. The qualifying clause in brackets — 'doing that thing quhilk appertenis to his charge' — can at most, therefore, imply a right to political resistance, but not to freedom of conscience and religion.

Also directed against Anabaptist theologians, perhaps, is the condemnation of the heresy of those who deny 'the Eternitie of his (Christ's) Godheade, eythir the veritie of his humane nature' (Ch. 6). But the only examples cited by the Confession here are taken from early church history.

In content, the *Confessio Belgica* (1561) is substantially the same as its predecessors. But unlike them it refers to the Anabaptists by name. In Article 18, for example, it attacks 'the heresy of the Anabaptists, who deny that Christ assumed human flesh from His mother'. The background to this polemic is the controversy between Micronius and Menno Simons about the incarnation and redemption through Christ. This controversy is also referred to in Calvin's *Institutio.*

The two Articles of the *Confession de Foy* condemning the rebaptism of the already baptized and the rejection of infant baptism are brought together in a single article in the *Confessio Belgica* which condemns those *'qui unico et semel suscepto baptismo contenti non sunt; ac praeterea, baptismum infantium, fidelibus parentibus natorum damnant'* (Art. XXXIV), 'who are not content with the baptism once and for all received and even condemn the baptism of infants born to believing parents'. Reference is made to the covenant sign of circumcision as justification here and it is emphasized that the redemption accomplished through Christ also embraces children.

Article XXXVI of the *Confessio Belgica* is substantially the same as Article 40 of the *Confession de Foy,* except that it specifically mentions the Anabaptists. *'Quamobrem Anabaptistas aliosque homines seditiosos detestamur, atque in universum omnes eos, qui supremas Dominationes et Magistratus reiiciunt, iustitiam evertunt, bonorum communionem inducunt, atque honestatem, quam Deus inter homines stabilivit, confundunt'* ('Wherefore we deprecate the Anabaptists and other factious persons and in general all those who reject the supreme authorities and magistrates, overthrow justice, introduce the community of possessions, and bring disorder into the order of mutual considerateness established by God among men'). At the same time, however, the *Confessio Belgica* demands freedom for evangelical preaching — over against the Spanish authorities.

The purpose of these three Calvinistic confessions of faith is the edification of the church. They seek to provide as complete a summary of the evangelical faith as possible. At the same time they insist on the national loyalty of the church or the church's solidarity with the nation. The Anabaptists are condemned wherever they deny these two concerns in essential respects.

6. *The Confessio Helvetica posterior.* The *Second Helvetic Confession* was produced in 1561/1562 by Heinrich Bullinger, Zwingli's successor in Zurich, in the first instance as a personal statement of faith. In 1566 it attained official status. With this document, the production of Reformed confessions of faith in the 16th century comes to a close. What Bullinger sought to do was to provide a summary of 'the orthodox faith and catholic doctrine of the pure Christian religion', in accord with the churches of the nations of Christendom and with the ancient apostolic Church, and in this way to bring about peace and concord among the churches.

What the *Helvetica posterior* did actually serve to promote was the inner unification of the Reformed churches. At the same time it marked the dividing lines more sharply in other directions. A clear division is made not only over against the Roman Catholic Church but also, by direct or indirect repudiations, over against the Anabaptists. In addition to this, the *Second Helvetic Confession* took care to define its position over against Jews and Mohammedans, pagans, philosophers, and the ancient church heresies. Henceforth the Anabaptists are considered to be definitively divorced from the true church and its teaching. They are even more severely condemned than the Roman Catholic Church. In respect of the Anabaptists, the *Helvetica posterior* speaks of condemnation (damnamus), whereas a milder term is used in respect of the Roman Catholic Church; the papacy's usurpation of power is 'not approved' *(non probamus).* The Roman Catholic Church is not regarded as heretical, for it does indeed stand on the basis of the Ancient Church of which the Reformation considers itself the continuation.

There are indirect as well as direct repudiations of the Anabaptists in the *Second Helvetic Confession.* We take first the condemnations which undoubtedly include the Anabaptists but do not mention them explicitly. Chapter II states the principle that Scripture is to be interpreted contextually and according to the rule of faith and love. Chapter VII rejects the doctrine of the sleep of the soul after death. Chapter XI repudiates the doctrine that in the end all are saved, as well as 'the Jewish dreams' *(Iudaica somnia)* of an earthly messianic kingdom. In the same chapter, the Confession rejects christological heresies in connection with the incarnation and the redemption by Christ. Chapter XXII condemns separation from the church and the holding of clandestine meetings. Chapter XXIX rejects polygamy. Reference was already made at the beginning of this paper to the two passages in which the Anabaptists are explicitly condemned (see p. 42): in Chapter XX on Holy Baptism and in Chapter XXX on the Civil Authority.

The section on Baptism stresses its character as 'sign of initiation into the People of God'. The repudiation of the Anabaptists in this section is based not merely on their view and their practice of baptism but is much more comprehensive. 'We also condemn the Anabaptists in respect of other doctrines of theirs which contain features contrary to the Word of God'. The concluding sentence of this Chapter reads almost like a final summary: *'Non sumus ergo Anabaptistae, neque com eis in ulla re ipsorum communicamus'* ('We are not Anabaptists nor do we have any common ground with them in their cause').

The chapter *'De Magistratu'* (ch. XXX) starts from the fact that it is God Himself who has instituted civil authority. In the ideal case, it will be a 'most useful and outstanding member of the Church' who bears responsibility for government. The Christian magistrate has to stand up for religion. The fact that the power of the sword has been entrusted to the magistrate may mean that this magistrate must in certain cases apply the death penalty to blasphemers. The incorrigible heretic must be kept in check by force. In serious emergencies, the magistrate may, in God's name, even wage war in order to save the nation. 'We condemn the Anabaptists who deny not only that a Christian may hold public office but also that the magistrate may justly put anyone to death or wage war, or has any right to exact an oath etc.' The section deals in the first instance exclusively with the Anabaptists and their mistaken view of civil authority. At the end of the section the condemnation is extended. Rebels and those disloyal to the State are the subject of a general condemnation.

The quarrel of the *Helvetica posterior* with the Anabaptists rests on two premises. Anabaptists deviate from the true Church by their erroneous view of Scripture and by their denial of the unity of Christian life and civil life. Bullinger tries to demonstrate that the Anabaptists must be condemned because of these two deviant views. The *Helvetica posterior* establishes the attitude of the Reformed Church towards the Anabaptists in the direction of the State Church.

7. *The Westminster Confession of Faith (1648).* Like the later Reformed confessions generally, the *Westminster Confession* contains no explicit condemnation of the Anabaptists. This certainly does not mean that the later Reformed confessions did not continue the anti-Anabaptist tradition. Even the *Westminster Confession* (Chap. XXVIII) clearly presents a doctrine of infant baptism which is basically the same as that of the *Helvetica posterior*. Even the view of the civil authority (Chapters XXII and XXIII) reappears unchanged. The State's obligation is explicitly emphasized: 'It is his (i.e. the

civil magistrate's) duty to take order that unity and peace be preserved in the Church... that all blasphemies and heresies be suppressed, all corruptions and abuses in worship and discipline prevented and reformed and all ordinances of God duly settled, administered and observed'.

The *Westminster Confession* shows the extent to which the positions developed in the controversy with the Anabaptists had hardened and become a firm element in the Reformed tradition.

II. CONFESSIONS OF FAITH AND THE CONFESSION OF THE REFORMED CHURCHES TODAY

What significance do these findings have for the relationship of the Reformed Churches to the Mennonite Churches today? What do we make of our forebears' repudiation of the Anabaptists? Every Reformed Christian is intuitively aware that a new situation has arisen. Despite the statements of the Reformers we are now ready to seek not only dialogue, but also communion in worship and witness with our fellow Mennonite Christians. What is the appropriate evaluation of this spontaneous inclination?

We are committed to our own tradition. The views of the Reformers and confessions of faith of the 16th and 17th centuries are still important for us. We cannot ignore their witness as if it were not in some measure at least decisive for us. If we arrive at insights and conclusions different from those of our forebears, we have to be able to assume responsibility for these different views in their presence. What considerations should be mentioned?

1. *Openness.* Most of the Reformed confessions of faith are characterized by a certain openness. Undoubtedly they set out to define the content of the Gospel seriously and conscientiously. But their authors realize that what they say is not necessarily the last word on the subject. As a rule, they expressly state their willingness to receive better instruction in the light of Holy Scripture. In actual practice, this openness has led the Reformed Church to raise fresh questions; even when these concerned issues which seemed already settled by the confessions of faith. They did not commit themselves to their confessions of faith in such a way as to exclude new developments. The confessions are recognized and respected as important testimonies, but it is also necessary to wrestle afresh again and again with contemporary questions in each new situation in the light of the witness of Holy Scripture. Just as the Reformation was itself a movement, so too the Reformed tradition remains a movement which, in fellowship with the Reformers, continues to probe afresh into the meaning of the Gospel.

This qualification, this proviso, is already to be found in Zwingli. He submits his *Fidei ratio* to the decision of the whole church 'insofar as it decides in obedience to and inspired by God's Word and Spirit'.

A similar statement is found in the introduction to the statement of the *Bern Synod:* 'But if something is forthcoming from our pastors or from any other quarter which leads us closer to Christ and which, in the light of God's Word, is more conducive to general concord and Christian love than the opinion here set down, we will gladly accept it and not obstruct the movement of the Holy Spirit, Who drives us not backwards but always forwards towards the likeness of Christ Jesus our Lord.' The primary emphasis in both these statements is that better insights, insights more in accord with the Gospel of Christ, can only derive from the witness of Holy Scripture. At the same time, however, both statements show an awareness that every confession of faith must submit itself to the judgement of the whole church. The objections of others are always taken seriously, as a matter of course.

Similar remarks are also found in later confessions of faith. In the introduction to the *Second Helvetic Confession,* for example, it is declared: *'Ante omnia vero protestamur nos semper esse paratissimos, omnia et singula hic a nobis proposita, si quis requirat, copiosus explicare, denique meliora ex verbo Dei docentibus, non sine gratiarum actione, et cedere et obsequi in Domino, Cui laus et gloria!'* ('Above all, however, we testify that we are always entirely willing to explain more fully each and every proposition here set forth, if anyone requests this, and finally, if taught better things from the Word of God, to yield and obey, not unthankfully, in the Lord, to Whom be praise and glory!').

What is the significance of this basic openness for the rejection of the Anabaptists? It can only mean, surely, that a new discussion on the basis of Holy Scripture is always not only possible but even mandatory. Not only is dialogue not in contradiction to the confessions; it is actually required by them. Mennonites profess explicitly their submission to the witness of Scripture. The condition for dialogue is therefore met. The encounter is governed by the promise that it can 'lead us closer to Christ'; it is also mandatory because the Church can never become resigned to division but always see it as a spur to ask afresh what is 'more conducive to general concord and Christian love'.

2. *Changing convictions.* Do not the Reformed churches need, however, to take a step further than this general consideration? Are they not required to wrestle specifically and in detail with those confessional statements about the Anabaptists? Do we not have to examine them and explain in so many words how far they are still true today?

This is a process which is undoubtedly already going on in the Reformed churches. It began when some Reformed churches sought to relieve these statements of their discriminatory character. A particularly important role was played here by the Presbyterian

Church of the United States. In 1788, this church committed itself in principle to mutual tolerance and, in view of the separation of Church and State in the USA, urged the state to cherish the church of our common Lord without privileging any one Christian denomination over any other. And, since 1879, the point is made in statements by Presbyterian churches in the United States that no article of the confession of faith is to be thought of as an incentive to or justification for intolerance or persecution or utilized for such a purpose.

The questioning of the repudiations, however, goes even deeper. It has become obvious that the conditions of Christian witness have changed. The firm convictions on which the repudiations rested can no longer be maintained today without qualification. The Reformed churches have been forced to admit, therefore, that it is no longer possible to conduct the discussion today on the basis of the convictions formerly held. And this admission leads inescapably to the conclusion that already then, in the 16th and 17th centuries, the Anabaptists championed insights to which more serious heed should have been paid. Three observations are particularly important here:

First, the Reformed churches have come to take a more nuanced view of the authority of Holy Scripture in modern times. The Reformers appealed to the witness of Holy Scripture to justify their message and their criticism of the conditions then prevailing in the Church. Subsequent developments led them to develop the Scripture principle. Scripture alone is the source of knowledge. Scripture alone is the basis for church doctrine. The transition to such statements about Scripture is already effected at an early date. The *First Helvetic Confession* (1536) begins by affirming that the whole Bible is the only basis of doctrine; then follows the affirmation that Holy Scripture is to be interpreted by Holy Scripture. This conception remains the decisive one even in the later confessions, above all in the *Westminster Confession*.

It has been supposed that this formulation of the Scripture principle was prompted, in part at least, by the controversy with the Anabaptists. The Reformers tried to establish the validity of the witness of the whole Bible, in opposition to Anabaptist exegesis which they regarded as selective. We must be guided by the whole of Scripture; it cannot be a matter of preferring individual biblical passages.

Today, however, the Reformed churches are no longer in a position to maintain the Scripture principle in the form in which it was expressed in the classic confessions. Using the methods of historical criticism, biblical scholarship has made it clear that the witness of Scripture reflects an historical development. It does indeed attest the *one* Gospel but it does so in a variety of voices. The Scriptures give us a picture of how the Church of the first century attested the Gospel in the light of its situation at that time. They invite us to undertake this same task afresh today. In every generation the Church must reach accord as to the witness required by the *one* Gospel. This new way of handling the Scriptures is explicitly recognized in more recent Reformed confessions of faith.

Does this not mean, however, that the Reformed and Mennonite churches must now conduct the discussion about the authority of Scripture in a new way?

Second, the fronts, too, have shifted in the question of Church and State. The basis for the Reformed condemnation of the Anabaptists on this issue was the assumption that Church and State have to cooperate in close alliance. Certainly the Church was to be distinguished, but not divorced from the State. The two regiments were closely interrelated. The Reformation was not simply the renewal of the Church; it was also a renewal of political life. So the State had a responsibility for the organized life of the Church, because the witness of the Church was of vital importance for the whole of society and its sound development. It was not enough, therefore, for the Reformation to produce merely a revived religious community. It had to envision the whole of society.

Developments in recent centuries have challenged the validity of this assumption in a variety of ways. The discrepancy between the witness of the Gospel, on the one hand, and the values underlying the growth of society, on the other, has become increasingly palpable. The vision of the Reformers continues to be important in the sense that the Church's witness must always encompass society in its entirety. It has become clear, however, that for the sake of a clear witness, what is required is a Church which is more clearly aware of its evangelical mission. It must be so constituted that it can stand up to the State.

Above all, there has been a rediscovery of the importance of the witness for peace. A Church would become savorless salt if it were not to question closely, for example, the right to wage war (*Helvetica posterior,* see p. 50 above). The questionable character of the alliance of the Church with the State, with the ruling power and the dynamic of its interests, has become more palpable today than ever.

The conditions therefore exist for a new discussion of the proper witness of the church in society.

Finally, as a result of these two changes, new fronts have also emerged in the question of baptism. Many Reformed churches have come to realize that it is not so easy to justify from the New Testament the baptism of the infant children of believing parents as the Reformers supposed. Above all, however, increasing secularization has made the general baptism of children even more questionable than it was to begin with. How a church which is aware of its mission can ever come into existence if this practice is retained becomes a serious question.

These developments have not led the Reformed churches to call the baptism of infants into question completely. But they have become far more open and receptive to the practice of believers' baptism, and are usually ready to regard both forms of baptism as complementary ways of reception into the community of faith.

3. *A new situation.* As the convictions underlying the Reformed repudiation of the Anabaptists have changed, a new situation has arisen in respect of the relationship with Mennonites. The Reformed churches can state openly today that they have been led beyond the stage of their earlier insights. This in no way diminished their fidelity to the witness of the Reformers and the confessions of faith formulated in earlier times. As they seek to bear this witness today, they see that the fronts are not to be drawn today in the same way that they were previously, and indeed that even then, under more propitious circumstances, perhaps they need not have been drawn in the way they were.

The confessions of the Reformation are framed in such a way that every generation must ask anew how it is to formulate the message entrusted to it. It is, therefore, an act of fidelity to the heritage of the Reformation when also the present generation tackles this task. The Gospel needs to be expressed and attested anew. Cannot Reformed Christians and Mennonite Christians set their hands to this task together in a new way today?

Suggested reading
The texts of the confessions referred to are found in:
— E.F.K. Müller, *Die Bekenntnisschriften der reformierten Kirche,* Leipzig, 1903.
— Wilhelm Niesel, *Bekenntnisschriften und Kirchenordnungen der nach Gottes Wort reformierten Kirche,* Zollikon-Zürich, 1938.
— *Der Berner Synodus von 1532, Vol. I:* Edition of the original text with a modern German translation, ed. by the Research Seminar for Reformation Theology under Gottfried W. Locher, Neukirchen, 1984; Vol. II: Studies and Essays (due to appear shortly).

Individual essays:
— Willem Balke, *Calvin and the Anabaptist Radicals,* Grand Rapids, Michigan 1981.
— Heinold Fast, *Heinrich Bullinger und die Täufer,* No. 7 in the series published by the Mennonite Historical Association, 1959.
— Alasdair Heron, ed. *The Westminster Confession in the Church Today,* Edinburgh 1982.
— Rudolf Pfister, *Kirchengeschichte der Schweiz 2,* Zurich 1974.
— John H. Yoder, *Die Gespräche zwischen Täufern und Reformatoren in der Schweiz 1523-1538,* No. 6 in the series published by the Mennonite Historical Association, 1962.

A Mennonite view on the Reformed Condemnations

By HEINOLD FAST

1. *'Not rejection of those who believe differently but discernment of the spirits'.*

The preceding chapter is permeated by the tension between criticism and affirmation of the judgments on the Anabaptists found in Reformation writings. This is intrinsic in any testing of tradition. According to the paper, 'to the extent that these repudiations were used to justify the oppression and persecution of the (Ana)baptists, the Reformed churches must dissociate themselves from them'. On the other hand, the Reformed 'are committed to their own tradition' and may still after biblical examination reject *the teachings* of the Anabaptists, without the 'public accusations, executions, and banishments'. It is clear that earlier conflict will not be easily laid to rest, and the points of contention should not be pronounced insignificant. The distance from 16th century repudiations has its limits from the start.

I consider this to be integral. If we want to resume discussion of topics controversial then, our motivation should not be courtesy. As then, the question is, which truth will we confess, on what does our personal salvation and that of the world depend? But the preaching of the gospel makes not only salvation but also lostness recognizable, as truth reveals untruth. Rejection must for this reason be possible yet today; indeed, we will not be able to avoid it. But does this mean we must fall back into a state of reciprocal condemnation?

I would like to suggest a distinction which was not expressly named in the essay but is factually present in the argument: what people say or do may be deplorable, but they themselves are not. As I write this, I remember that the Anabaptists themselves were not far behind the Reformed in damning their opponents. Perhaps they were recalling the decisiveness with which Paul flung his anathema at the enemies of his theology of justification (Gal. 1:8f.); they forgot that this same Paul is very generous in other situations (Phil. 1:15-18) or differentiates between words or actions and the person who speaks or acts. For Christians, renunciation of persons of another persuasion is basically not permissible, although they are well aware of the divisive power of the word of God (Heb. 4:12).

2. *Holy Scripture as the foundation, not of self-justification, but of thinking together starting from the gospel.*

It is encouraging that the paper emphasizes the importance of Scripture for our discussion, particularly in reference to the openness of Reformed confessions. 'As a rule, (the authors of the confessions) expressly state their willingness to receive better instruction in the light of Holy Scripture.' Scripture is not only the basis of Christian confession but also challenges positions formerly adhered to. Holy Scripture not only makes new discussion possible but commands it.

We could become discouraged as we look back at the many discussions between Reformed and Anabaptists in the 16th century. Everyone always agreed that they wanted to be corrected by Holy Scripture. A few people were convinced and changed sides. But the confessions never came any closer. If the bare fact that conversation continued assumed a common foundation, the progress of the conversation must have disappointed both parties. Did the Bible not supply what was expected of it? Was this willingness to be corrected only a rhetorical exercise? In any case, the expectations that had been fastened to these conversations were unfulfilled — apparently already in early stages because of the ways the parties used Scripture. Must we fear the same results for discussions today?

It is for this reason that what the paper states concerning 'a more nuanced view of the authority of Holy Scripture' is important to us. As early as the 16th-century the Anabaptists did not accept the Reformed explanation of the differences between Reformed and Anabaptists as the contrast between contextual and selective exegesis. Contextual exegesis served as a formal principle which permitted citation of Old Testament proof texts; in the eyes of the Anabaptists, the *function* was selective, as, for example, in the justification of war. The concept of *one* gospel is helpful, with which the paper acknowledges the results of historical-critical research in seeking the essential content behind the many voices. 'Gospel' has to do primarily with Jesus Christ, his words and deeds, his life, and his mission. This already supplies the variety of voices preaching the gospel with the highest authority given in the Bible as the criteria of exegesis, namely, the authority they already claim and preach, Jesus Christ. But since Jesus Christ is to be understood only through many voices, we must listen to them in concert, those in the Bible as well as those in history and in the present. The discussion between confessions is not only desirable; it is necessary for knowing Jesus Christ. Biblical hermeneutics is dependent on an ecumenical ecclesiology and is at the same time one of its foundational pillars. We must remember this (but also not lose sight of discernment of spirits); we may not permit ourselves resignation in the face of past experiences.

3. *Not separatism or blind assimilation, but witness to the whole society.*

Numerous Anabaptist teachings which were rejected by the Reformed were controversial even among Anabaptists, and some were soon forgotten, as, for example, Melchior Hoffman's doctrine of the incarnation, which was so central for Menno Simons. But the most important question is still the relationship of church and state, even though the answer to this question has varied greatly in the course of history. The history of this topic traces the history of the theological self-understanding of the Mennonites. This is the legacy of the radical break with ruling powers, or, stated theologically, the tension between gospel and world.

Anabaptists considered authorities, people using the power of the sword, as representatives of the fallen creation ('world') as well as instruments of God for maintenance of a relative order. The apparent contradiction in this double standard was seldom accepted, and the Anabaptists themselves had difficulties in maintaining it. As a result, authorities either were depicted as devilish or were uncritically obeyed. As the 'Quiet in the Land' the Mennonites found economic success and earned a good reputation for genuine piety. But the power of the gospel for the whole of society was lost. In the end, many Mennonites had enough of such an existence and assimilated, having lost the power to discern the spirits.

The conclusion, that the church must 'envision the whole of society' and yet for the sake of its witness remember 'the discrepancy between the witness of the Gospel... and the values underlying the growth of a society,' formulates the lesson that Mennonites need to learn again, only they come to this assignment from the separatist side. For Reformed as well as for Mennonites, the essential questions today have nearly the same structure as they had over 460 years ago, when the Anabaptists and Zwingli separated. We can only affirm that 'the conditions... exist for a new discussion of the proper witness of the Church in society.'

4. *No over-valuation of the baptism question, but its appropriate place in the broader theological, especially ecclesiological, perspective.*

Looking back on the origin of the Anabaptist movement in the bosom of the Zurich Reformation, Zwingli regarded the question of infant or adult baptism as secondary. He accused the Anabaptists of making such a major issue of the baptism problem because they intended to found their own, separate church. Zwingli made the connection between the right use of the sacrament of baptism and the ecclesiological question, and especially with the question of the relationship between church and world. This was natural for him, since he himself tried to solve the question of baptism from ecclesiological perspectives. The form of baptism, an external matter, must be decided within the framework of church praxis in a society concerned for religious unity. This unity was challenged by the Anabaptists, and the call for believers' baptism was in fact an expression of this challenge, even if it was not so understood in its beginnings. Anyone wishing to return to this contention must broaden the theological perspective beyond the narrow sense of sacrament.

The essay does this when it speaks of new fronts emerging and mentions the factor of growing secularization. In view of secularization, Christians of people's churches have recognized that the church of Jesus Christ must be a confessing church and infant baptism is questionable. But new deliberations also among Mennonites are necessary. To be sure, we are descended from the tradition which began with a break with the *corpus christianum*. The Anabaptists considered nominal Christians heathen, despite their baptism as infants. But in the meanwhile we have slid into many different forms of socialization — the family church, the ethnic group, the economic achievers, or even only a part of the reservoir of the absolutely faithful servile. We are looking for ways out of such captivity, and new consideration of baptism plays a role, a secondary role as in the past. Of first importance is the question of how the church can be, not only preach, a witness for the kingdom of God in the worldly world. And yet again we conclude, out of the need in which we stand together with the Reformed, that it is time we engage in deeper conversation.

Dialogue in the Netherlands

As an aid and stimulation for conversation elsewhere, this section summarizes papers growing out of conversations in The Netherlands from 1975-1978.

Participating in the conversations were three theologians of the Netherlands Reformed Church, three of the Dutch Mennonite Brotherhood, two of the Reformed Churches in the Netherlands, two Baptist theologians, and one of the Christian Reformed Church.

After extensive exploratory discussions, the participants chose to reflect upon six themes. The final report, *Dopers-Calvinistisch Gesprek in Nederland* (Mennonite-Reformed Dialogue in The Netherlands) was published in 1982 by Boekencentrum in The Hague. The following summary treats the six topics addressed jointly by a Mennonite/Baptist theologian and by one from the Reformed tradition.

Theme I: THE COVENANT (by J. Reiling and W. van't Spijker)

The relationship between the old and new covenants was a central issue in the conversations. The Reformed tradition emphasizes, above all, the unity of the old and new covenants. Reformers such as Zwingli, Bucer, and Calvin have stated that substantially the same salvation and the same faith are at stake in the old and the new covenants; Abraham was a Christian before Christ. Therefore, it belongs to the essence of the covenant as a covenant of grace that the whole nation in its continuity of generations be included. This Old Testament datum applies to the Christian Church as well. It is within this context, corresponding to Old Testament circumcision, that the practice of infant baptism is upheld. Consequently, the course of the Church as a covenant people is described in Old Testament terms as walking before the Lord according to his commandments. For this reason there has traditionally been a fixed place in many Reformed liturgies for the weekly reading of the commandments.

Mennonites have traditionally emphasized, above all, the new aspect of the new covenant, and that this is the gift of the Holy Spirit. The Christian Church, unlike Israel, lives in the era following the pouring out of the Spirit. The walk of the Church is one according to the Spirit; the Church as a community of faith is not a community formed by a continuity of generations, but is formed in discontinuity through personal conversion and rebirth through the Spirit.

In reference to the concept of theocracy, the Reformed tradition has considered society as a whole in light of the demand and promise of the covenant. The Mennonite/Baptist tradition has emphasized the personal, free choice of the believer. Through this choice, a new people comes into being; this people of God holds a different position in respect to society from that which the Reformers thought it held.

In light of the above positions, biblical orientation on the covenant is important. In the Old Testament, we read first about God's covenant with Noah (Gen. 9) and with Abraham (Gen. 15 and 17). A basic element of the biblical concept of covenant is that God voluntarily enters into a commitment; it is He who has founded the covenant; fundamentally, it is unilateral. Abraham has only his faith which was 'reckoned to him as righteousness' (Gen. 15:6). He is asked to administer circumcision to all male descendants as a sign of the covenant symbolizing the act of faith in God's promise (Gen. 17:10).

The covenant between God and Israel at Sinai has a different structure. The concluding of this covenant implies the revelation of God's will in the Torah (Law). After Moses had read The Book of the Covenant to the people, they pledged obedience to what the Lord had spoken; the concluding of the covenant follows (Ex. 24:7-8). Henceforth, law and covenant are connected.

Covenant history in the Old Testament is the story of God's faithfulness and human unfaithfulness. Through the pronouncement of judgment there is promise of a new covenant. The link between covenant and Torah is not broken: 'I will put my law within them...' (Jer. 31:33-34).

In the New Testament there are several ways of continuing to deal with the Old Testament covenant. First, there is Paul's line of thought that the covenant with Abraham — or rather the promise to Abraham — has been fulfilled in Christ (Gal. 3:15-17). Here there is a direct line from the promise of salvation to Abraham to the fulfilment in Christ, the law being only an auxiliary that since Christ's coming can be abolished. What has already applied to Abraham, applies all the more in the new covenant — God's grace has been given and the only acceptable answer in return is faith.

Alongside the continuing line of the covenant with Abraham, there is the broken line of the Sinai covenant which was ruptured by the disobedience of Israel. In Christ a new start is made, a new covenant founded (see the words spoken at the Last Supper, Mark 14:24; I Cor. 11:25). This is presented impressively in Hebrews where the contrast between old and new covenant has been vigorously emphasized.

Finally, in a different connection, Paul contrasts the old covenant with the new one. He characterizes the old covenant by the letter, by death; and the new covenant by the Spirit, by life (II Cor. 3:6). Where there is no danger of the law being a second way of salvation apart from Christ, Paul qualifies the law as good and holy, to be obeyed in a way of life that is not sinful in nature but that is lived 'according to the Spirit' (Rom. 8:3).

The Reformed and Mennonite/Baptist traditions could usefully devote attention to the relationship between the covenant and the Lord's Supper. The Lord's Supper is the sign of God's prevenient grace, and the sign of conversion with rebirth. Both accents are present.

Theme II: WORD AND SPIRIT (by W. Balke and O.H. de Vries)

The relationship between Word and Spirit was a frequent discussion topic during our sessions. For a long time, it was quite usual to consider 16th century Anabaptists as fanatics (Schwärmer), seeing them wrongly as spiritualists who stated that the Spirit gave special revelations apart from the Word to true believers. There were, of course, at that time spiritualistic tendencies, but Mennonite/ Baptists never intended to detach Word from Spirit any more than did the Reformed.

In the Bible, Word and Spirit are indissolubly interrelated. Together they are instruments of God's creative action (Gen. 1:2-3; Ps. 33:6). Together they create history, the history of the new life of God's people. The Word is not only God's creating Word, but it is also the Word of His law; and (Ezek. 36:27) the Spirit is to bring about the miracle of obedience in Israel. Paul, too, deals with the creative work of the Spirit in the life of believers (II Cor. 3). Here Paul suggests (vs. 2, 14, 15) that the Word in its fullness is only known when, through the work of the Spirit, it becomes living practice.

The Mennonite/Baptist tradition never intended to separate Word and Spirit; the Reformed never intended totally including the Spirit in the Word (at most, Calvin spoke about the Spirit being 'more or less' included in the Word). Here, however, the two traditions have a difference of emphasis.

Cautiously speaking, we can say that according to Reformed tradition, the Spirit is, above all, the interpreter of the Word, whereas according to Mennonite/Baptist tradition, the Spirit, above all, makes the Word become reality in the life of the believer and in that of the congregation. More than the Anabaptists, the Reformed have always emphasized the inter-relatedness of Word and Spirit, the criteria for every appeal to the Spirit being in the Scripture. The Spirit has seen fit to bind itself to the Word so that the Word evoked by the Spirit is never without that Spirit. In their interpretation of the Bible, the Reformed valued scientific knowledge more than the Anabaptists did. The latter emphasized obedience to the Word as a condition for its understanding. Characteristically, the 16th century Anabaptist theologian Hans Denck said: 'I can grasp the truth in so far as I myself have been grasped by the truth.'

Reiterating, there are here only differences of emphasis. As to the relationship between Word and Spirit, essential differences have never existed between Reformed and Anabaptists.

Theme III: CHRISTOLOGY (by J. Veenhof and S. Voolstra)

The concept of Christology shows closely intertwining similarities and differences between Mennonite/Baptist and Reformed traditions. Emphatic differences can be described as follows: the Reformed put the accent on Christ, the Son of God, who became human in order to take the position of Mediator to reconcile those who belong to Him; the Anabaptists emphasized that Christ, the Son of God, became the New Being, who as predecessor of His followers, went the entire way of sanctification and obedience.

Sixteenth century Anabaptists such as Melchior Hoffman, Menno Simons, and Dirk Philips pointed out that in the text 'the Word became flesh' (John 1:14), it is not stated that the Word 'adopted' the flesh. Thus, they rejected the view that in His incarnation Christ adopted Mary's flesh. They also rejected the concept of Christ having had a dual nature (human and divine) combined in one person. For them, the total newness was of highest importance. Moreover, they readily used the contrast presented by Paul (I Cor. 15:47) when he spoke of the 'first man being of the dust of the earth, the second man being from heaven'. Accordingly, they emphasized the New Being's pre-eminently divine origin. For Anabaptists there was an unbridgeable gulf between the sinfulness of human nature and the New Being which was Christ. Becoming a Christian was considered a new act of creation from and by the Spirit. Justification and sanctification were closely interrelated; for God, no one is 'justified' whose faith does not bear the fruits of the Spirit. Anabaptists guarded against Christ's priestly office being overemphasized at the expense of His prophetic ministry and His royal office.

One of the distinguishing marks of Anabaptist Christology is its emphasis on the passion of Christ that is a demonstration of God's love calling for love in return, that again in its turn does not shun sacrifice and suffering which results from the world's misjudgment and hatred. Thus, the willingness to undergo suffering has its roots in Christology.

All this is no superficial moralism. Christ as the absolutely New Being born of God makes rebirth possible. In Christ, the believer's newness does not proceed from human nature that has been totally corrupted by sin, but from God Himself, through His Word and Spirit. The believer is reborn into the membership of the fellowship of believers that represents the new creation in a fallen world, and in this fellowship there is, with a view to continuing sanctification, the necessity of discipline.

Unlike the Anabaptists, the Reformed maintained that Christ adopted a true human, though sinless, nature from the flesh and blood of Mary. They held that in order to become Mediator, Christ had to participate in and become united with that which He was to liberate from the power of sin. In this way he first represented the 'old' being who was sinful and alienated from God. In their opinion, grace is not the opposite of the natural and human as such, but carries with it the restoration of human nature. From early times they emphasized Christ as Mediator, truly God and truly Man.

Nevertheless, the Reformed also constantly emphasize the necessity of sanctification. Here they agree with the Anabaptists although without the characteristic Anabaptist accent on suffering. Like the Anabaptists, the Reformed state that the Christian in his new way of life does not exist alone; he needs the spiritual community and is responsible for it. They preferably speak of 'unity with Christ'; but at the same time, they point out that this unity implies the community of Christians as well.

Even though both traditions considered discipline as necessary in the congregation, their method of exercising it was different. The Reformed always strongly felt that man, sanctified in Christ, remains susceptible to evil. The Heidelberg Catechism (answer 114) says even that those who are most sanctified have, in this life, only a small beginning of obedience. Today, however, the Reformed admit that a statement like this is inadequate in view of what Paul says on new life in Christ. Because of 'realistic considerations' Anabaptists did not wish in any way to detract from the radicality of renewal. Here there is room for a beneficial disturbance among the Reformed, though the Mennonites/Baptists of today could learn much too on this point from their own 16th century forefathers.

However, considering the strong impulse to seek merit, it might be advantageous to take more note of the Reformed emphasis on justification by free grace with Christ as Mediator identifying Himself with the sinner.

Theme IV: THE CHURCH (by A. Geense and J.A. Oosterbaan)
In the act of faith man looks away from himself; he looks at Christ, at God. Hence, to look towards Christ away from itself is characteristic of the church that owes its existence to his presence. When matter-of-course reality in the life of the church is heavily disrupted as during the Reformation, it is inevitable that people once again begin to think critically about the characteristic features of the Church. In this context discussion between the Anabaptist

and the Reformed tradition played an important role. The Anabaptist tradition questions whether, in reforming the Church, Luther and Calvin stopped short of what they set out to do. Did they not, like Rome, work with the intention of structuring an institution including all inhabitants of the State rather than assembling the community of believers as a brotherhood? Within the context of current ecumenism, this is an important issue. It looks as though questions raised during the Reformation have lost little of their relevance. We are now experiencing a rapid, undeniable destruction of all elements and thoughts of a 'national' church that had continued to remain after the Reformation.

Ecclesiological contrasts become readily apparent when one traces the origins of the Reformed and Anabaptist views of the Church within the total reflection on the faith of each group. It is common for the Reformed tradition to deal first with the Church, afterwards with personal faith. Karl Barth also maintains this order and Calvin called the Church 'mother' of the believers. The Reformed view of the origin of the Church as preceding the origin of personal faith has its roots in Jesus' cross and resurrection. It is pointed out that according to the New Testament, the Spirit has primarily been given to the believers' community as a whole, and in this way to those who by baptism are personally incorporated in the community.

The Anabaptist tradition rejects the view of the community (congregation, church) being an outward means of faith. It is quite the reverse; they hold that the community of believers is the (immediate) fruit of the Spirit. The spiritual community originates as the unity of all believers in Christ. It is not by a church, an outward institute, that believers are bound together, but by Christ Himself who is the unity of those who believe. Consequently, this results in a more democratic form of government in the congregational community than does the synodal form resulting from Reformed ecclesiology.

Anabaptist tradition is also critical of the Reformed doctrine of covenant and their speaking of the Church as 'the People of God'. Reformed ecclesiology prefers having its origins beginning with Israel, and there is a question as to identifying 'Church' and 'People' (as in Israel 'People' and community of faith were identical). The similarity with Israel is rather that of being elected and called by God to proclaim, as a community of faith, His name in the midst of all nations and to demonstrate how people can live together on earth according to God's purpose. In the Church this is the issue at stake; here both traditions fully agree.

The Mennonites/Baptists correctly indicate that discipleship is a necessary distinguishing mark of Christian life. For believers, this means being conformed to the likeness of Christ. It is for this purpose that the Spirit, working on the basis of the accomplished salvation, recreates human life. Calvin, too, in the context of pneumatology, gives much attention to sanctification. Both the Reformed and Anabaptist traditions agree in considering discipline as one of the distinguishing marks of the true Church.

To be sure the two traditions have differing opinions on the limits of church membership. The Reformed tradition has always had difficulties in setting these precisely. One has the conviction that in this era it is not yet possible to separate effectively 'weeds and wheat', and that the covenant reaches wider than its appropriation by faith. Mennonites/Baptists describe this as half-heartedness. The necessity for daily renewal of sanctification can be obscured. Here, the quality of the spiritual community is at stake. However, since the quality of the community is nothing more than the proclamation of God's boundless love, it remains difficult to draw lines.

The Reformed tradition has always vigorously held to the view that the Church is an institution with fixed rules on faith and government. Anabaptist tradition had little interest in this and feared that the institution might obstruct the free working of the Spirit. However, the institutional Church is in itself not unspiritual. Every transport needs channels, so the Spirit uses channels as well, but remains unbound by the channels it uses. The Anabaptist emphasis on the free working of the Spirit may here be of help to the Reformed tradition.

This might be applicable, too, concerning the Reformed tradition of maintaining an ordained ministry, though this is not meant as a denial of the priesthood of believers. Reformed opinion holds that it is more the assembly than the individual person who bears the ministry. In all likelihood, there is less difference than there seems. The 'Kirk Session' or presbytery is in itself, as it were, a small community representative of the whole, whereas the small Mennonite/Baptist congregation in itself, as it were, is the 'Kirk Session'. Essentially, the congregation is a Christocratic brotherhood, and more importantly, it is a community of believers. It is here that Anabaptist tradition can make a definite contribution, and can reinforce those Congregational insights which are already within the Reformed family.

Theme V: BAPTISM (K. Blei and J. Reiling)
The Reformed tradition has principally upheld the legitimacy of infant baptism; the Anabaptists have principally rejected it. This has always appeared to be one of the most obvious controversies between Mennonites/Baptists and Reformed, but currently there is a growing mutual respect towards one another's views on baptism. In essential aspects they appear to agree.

They agree that baptism marks the transition from the 'old' way of life to the 'new' life-in-Christ. By baptism one is brought into relationship with Christ, incorporated, as it were (Rom. 6). God in Christ works through the Spirit in the one who is baptized. Baptism is first and foremost an act that one undergoes: one *is* baptized. It is the Lord who through baptism adds to the community (Acts 2:41, 47). However, transition to a new life in Christ does not take place passively. The person baptized turns about, directing himself/herself towards Christ and towards the community of faith; willingly he/she undergoes baptism and begins a new life. Thus, baptism and faith indissolubly belong together. Together they are the expression of the new life breaking through in the midst of the old world.

Baptism is a sign, not an act of magic nor an automatically self-effective means of salvation. Being more than just a reference, it is the incorporation into the body of Christ that takes place in baptism (Rom. 6). What happened in Christ 'there and then' for the salvation of humankind, is 'here and now' in baptism given to humans by the Holy Spirit in such a way that it is willingly accepted. The discussion as to whether or not baptism is an explanatory (illustrative) sign or an active causative means presupposes an incorrect dilemma. Theologically, Paul speaks of baptism by water and baptism by the Spirit as coinciding (I Cor. 12:13). According to Acts, they do not always coincide in time (Acts 8:14-17; 10:44-48; 19:5-6). That baptism as such and the gift of the Spirit are not identical is quite clear, but there is a relationship; where baptism has been administered, the gift of the Spirit is forthcoming, and where the Spirit has been received, baptism is the logical consequence.

Since baptism and personal faith belong indissolubly together they cannot be interpreted individualistically. One who is baptized is incorporated into the body of Christ which is the Church. But it is true of course, that in baptism it is precisely the individual — not the community — who receives salvation. The New Testament seems always to presuppose this.

Baptism on personal confession of faith is the most natural means of baptizing. The traditional Reformed confessions on baptism also take believers' baptism as their point of departure. Sacraments are considered to serve the strengthening of faith that has been created by the Word (*Heidelberg Catechism,* ans. 65, 66). Using this definition, the Catechism first deals extensively with baptism as such and finishes with infant baptism being treated in one question-answer at the end. In this context, suddenly the covenant terminology is used and infant baptism is defended with the argument that in the New Testament baptism has replaced circumcision. Curiously enough, in the preceding section on baptism, this terminology has not been used. The traditional Reformed baptism liturgy, however, does use the covenant terminology from the beginning, but here again, only the last paragraph deals explicitly with baptism as infant baptism. Today, parents who are members of the Reformed tradition and do not wish to have their child baptized because they prefer believers' baptism, should no longer be considered (be it only implicitly) as having failed to execute their parental duty.

The fact of God's saving initiative is often used in defending infant baptism. Undeniably God's grace precedes human faith. This is also confessed in the Mennonite/Baptist tradition. As such, it is no compelling argument in favour of or against a special baptismal practice. Not even in the Reformed tradition does it serve as such an argument where, in principle, only children of believers as 'included in the covenant' are baptized.

In defending the practice of infant baptism one cannot directly appeal to the New Testament. Presumably, this practice was adopted after gradual development when, during the era of Constantine, Church and nation increasingly overlapped. However, as a post-biblical development, it is not necessarily wrong. Pastoral motives may have advanced the introduction of infant baptism; these same pastoral motives challenge us to a new reflection. The period of the 'nation-church' and of the Christian society is past. Therefore the time when infant baptism was practised as self-evident is past as well. The baptismal candidate may perhaps once again run risks.

About the considerations above, Reformed and Mennonites/Baptists appear to be in agreement; nevertheless, there are still some differing views. The Reformed partner will not go so far as to agree with the Mennonite/Baptist radical rejection of infant baptism. He emphasizes that the faith of the Church precedes the faith of the individual as the soil in which it is rooted, as the environment in which it can and must prosper. He fears that in radically rejecting infant baptism, an individualistic faith will develop and bring with it an overemphasis on the human aspect of confession before baptism, at the expense of the aspect of grace that is present.

In turn, Baptists/Mennonites willingly acknowledge the blessing that Christian family life radiates. However, this is still, in their thinking, not a legitimization of infant baptism. They emphasize that personal responsibility should not be obscured by 'the faith of the Church'. They fear that this is the inevitable consequence of infant baptism. This is what makes it so difficult for them to recognize the baptizing of children as true baptism.

Theme VI: THE MESSIANIC WAY OF LIFE (by C. Augustijn and H. B. Kossen)

From its early origins, the Reformed considered the Anabaptist movement a movement of protest that did not leave society unaffected. Contrastingly, the mainstream of the Reformation was inclined to identify with the established social order. However, the critical distance from government and society, which in former times was characteristic of Anabaptists, can be currently found in modern form throughout Christianity. Since this concept has strongly gained influence, Mennonites/Baptists and Reformed are able here to agree about some fundamental views.

The western world of which we are a part is still essentially organized according to the principles of free enterprise and is dominated by a continuing conflict of interests in which also Christians are involved. Confessing Jesus as Lord in a world such as ours means choosing a messianic way of life, making peace as Jesus the Messiah came to make peace.

As the Anointed of that God who had revealed Himself as Liberator of the poor and oppressed, Jesus could do nothing but devote Himself to their needs, thus realizing God's purpose for Israel and the nations. This could not help but bring Jesus into conflict with the powers of the establishment, for he did not conceal societal antagonisms. Rather he exposed antagonisms by explicitly telling the rulers and the wealthy that they should convert from their godless practices. Since he, nevertheless, refused to turn against them with violence, he purchased His solidarity with the poor and oppressed with his death by surrendering without resistance to the violence of the rulers. Thus, he came to bring peace — peace with all! As a result, the congregation came into existence as the first fruit of that peacemaking, and is precisely thus an instrument in the progress of the messianic work of liberation.

Those confessing Jesus as Lord are, in so doing, united to a community where their belonging by birth to a certain class or nation becomes less important. For in the new community, a common stand is taken against all divisive social powers. Together, in obedience to the Lord, Christians should participate in a socio-economic order where the struggle for life is not fought at the expense of others, but fully together and on behalf of one another. Today, unlike in Paul's time, the community can find possibilities for this. As an alternative community, it will participate in the progress of the peacemaking activity of the Messiah. The struggle for a new socio-economic order will have to be linked to a policy of confrontation with all those powers that have an interest in continuing the social order as we know it today. In this realm of struggle, we can place such examples as the World Council of Churches' programme to combat racism and many of the activities in our own country sponsored by the Netherlands Council of Churches and related organizations such as the Inter-Church Peace Council (I.K.V.). Where churches understand this concept of community, the existing division within the Church of Christ is painful.

Important differences continue to remain concerning the manner in which the congregation should give form to its responsibility towards the social order as a whole. The Anabaptist conception of responsibility clearly differs from the mainline interpretation which presupposes that a congregation that singularly practices Jesus' commandment to love one's neighbour inclusive of one's enemy fails in its responsibility to the world. Because of the presence of evil in the world and in humankind, even Christians are forced to resort to using the sword to restrain this evil and thus participate in the responsibility of the secular authorities for the social order.

According to the Anabaptist understanding, congregational responsibility for the world should take concrete form in faithfulness to the way prepared and taught by Jesus. This means that the congregation will leave the protecting of the social order with the use of violence to others, namely to the secular authorities. That the following of Christ definitely includes social engagement follows what has already been written above about the messianic practices of Jesus.

As already described, the Mennonite/Baptist position emphasizes the peculiar responsibility of Christians, whereas the Reformed emphasizes the fact itself of Christians as living in society being indeed co-responsible for that society. However, the time may come when a Christian, for the sake of Christ, must refuse all cooperation; if this refusal comes too early, then he is co-responsible for the fostering of evil.

Mennonites/Baptists consider the Christian's life as almost entirely determined by his/her life within the fellowship of believers. The Reformed view accepts the fact that the Christian actually lives in both worlds and that the task of the Christian does not always coincide with that of a citizen. This is closely connected with the fact that within the Anabaptist movement, the eschatological implication is felt more clearly and intensely than within the Reformed tradition. The Reformers tried to channelize the eschatological tension (e.g. Luther's doctrine of the 'Two Kingdoms' or the doctrine of the 'Twofold Justice' i.e. in society and Church by Zwingli), but as a result, very often totally neutralized it.

Editorial note:
*   The proper witness of the church in society is a central issue in Mennonite and Reformed churches.   Often today as is amply illustrated in this booklet, the discussion focuses on the witness for peace. What does obedience to Christ's Lordship mean today for Christians in response to the call from the world for peace?   Both Mennonites and Reformed have recently spoken to this question.   Several of these statements follow.*

Mennonite World Conference

Conference Message
The Ninth Mennonite World Conference
Curitiba, Brazil
July 18-23, 1972

The Ninth Mennonite World Conference assembled at Curitiba, Brazil, July 18-23, 1972, with joy in our hearts and great thankfulness to God. He has granted us, as Mennonites and Brethren in Christ from all over the world, another gathering which has contributed greatly to the understanding of God's gift of reconciliation to the world in his Son, our Lord Jesus Christ.

As God's children and Mennonite Churches we have been challenged to cooperate in His work of reconciliation with new understanding of the dimensions of this task in our personal relationships, in relationships among our churches and among all peoples.

We rejoice in the growing involvement of representatives from Asia, Africa, and Latin America and minority communities of North America. We confess that the Church is truly whole only when every brother and sister can share fully and equally regardless of race or class or nation.

In this spirit we call our churches to fresh obedience in being and becoming God's people in truth, people who are brought together only by the grace of our Lord Jesus Christ.

From this conference we come with this message to our churches, to all who love our Lord Jesus Christ and who believe that their salvation and that of the whole world is in His name, and to all the peoples . Through the blessing of the Holy Spirit, we feel that God will continue the work He has begun in us, and that He will use our churches and all those who belong to them as agents of reconciliation for His great purpose.

We have experienced that the theme of our conference, 'Jesus Christ Reconciles', has opened our eyes anew to see the many dimensions this message has for our personal lives as Christians and for the society in which we are members. We have been strengthened in our responsibility towards the Lord who has given us the assurance of His grace in which alone we can trust and live. We have been strengthened in our responsibility towards the human needs and inadequacies that are rooted in alienation from God.

As the study of our theme in the plenary sessions, in the discussions afterwards, and in the different work groups progressed, some things became very clear to us.

I. That there does not have to be dissension between those in our family whose priority lies in the area of personal salvation, and those who see it as their primary duty to promote an active program of liberation from all forms of oppression and injustice, because both are aspects of the reconciling work of Christ. Nevertheless, there is dissension which calls for further repentance and reconciliation. The emphasis upon the total witness should lead us as a people to talk to each other understandingly and not to avoid each other. We have been convinced that the judgment of God comes to all of us because we have been reluctant to seek cooperation with all those Christians who want to work in the service of the Lord to attain that goal; and that we have not been critical enough in the evangelical evaluation of the means to reach it.

Second: that any witness for peace and for service to the needs of humanity, and the taking of a responsible and ciritical position should be the concern of the whole Church and all its members, so we cannot but promote this need for a personal involvement and decision by all our brothers and sisters wherever they live or work.

II. The message of reconciliation puts before the Church the reality that such a ministry can only be effective if the Church itself is a reconciling community. Forgiveness, repentance and suffering are the standards the Lord has set for His people. Only in the way of the Cross can we, in spite of our points of difference, find a real relationship. If we be servants to one another we can stand the test of our ability to serve the world. Our mind has to be reshaped to the mind of Christ. (Phil. 2).

We are deeply aware that conflicts will arise where the message of reconciliation is given and the ministry of reconciliation is working. We should not avoid them for these conflicts can be a means to test questions of truth, righteousness and freedom in the Gospel. We sense this as an appeal to our Mennonite churches, but it also implies our willingness to find this same relationship with all those Christians who share this faith that the Church of Jesus Christ should be instrumental in God's redeeming love for the world, and to make our ministry an expression of our common calling. We believe that in a divided world the united efforts of the churches in a testimony of word and deed for Jesus Christ is the will of God.

III. The message of reconciliation and its challenge comes to us in a world situation where conflicts of every kind are prevailing. Looking at this world, at family relationships, at social and economic discord, at racial strife, and at cruel warfare, we see the need of reconciliation as never before. But God has taken the initiative;

it is His will that we live in peace with Him and with one another. We strongly believe that God is working in this world and not only in the Church. In this faith we must proceed even if we need to recognize that our way cannot be any other than Christ's way, the way of the Cross.

As we have come together for this conference in Brazil, our thoughts go irrevocably to every country and people represented here as they try to fulfil their task in the great human family, but who mostly fall short of that task. As followers of Jesus Christ we do raise a prophetic voice against all exercise of violent repression, persecution and unjust imprisonment, torture and death, particularly for political reasons. We object to racism and other forms of discrimination whether in our churches or in society at large. As Mennonites who in their history have experienced what persecution represents, we feel that the thankfulness for a quiet and undisturbed life cannot close our eyes to the many inequities that are inherent to the social and economic structures of today's world. These structures have a violence in themselves and tend to lead people into dependency and exploitation. They cause the loss of self respect and identity, and they prevent the development of a community life. In a world in which the rich tend to become ever richer and the poor ever poorer, the Gospel of Jesus Christ cannot but point a way to a human dignity in which all may share. This human dignity finds its basis in the love of God for all alike.

As the manifestation of the Latin American setting of our conference and the wide participation of our churches in Africa and Asia, we are moved to stress this love and justice of God for all alike very strongly.

But we feel it as a cause of deep repentance, and we pray God that He might grant us that we in manifold ways on the smaller scale of our own surroundings, but also on a worldwide scale, show ourselves as reconcilers in the name of our Lord Jesus Christ who has broken down every wall of partition.

Adopted at the final session, Sunday evening, July 23, 1972.

An Agenda on Militarism and Development

The Findings Committee of the Tenth Assembly of the Mennonite World Conference (MWC, Wichita, 1978) called Mennonites to confess disobedience for 'our individualistic ways, our national idolatries, our imitating of dominant cultures and values, our indifferences toward a hungry world, our shyness in sharing the Good News of Christ, our timidity in confronting evil powers and principalities, our retreat from a courageous biblical Anabaptist faith, and our indifference to ominous and monstrous threats to the peace of the world'.

The MWC was a clear reminder to the churches of North America and Europe that we are members of 'one world'. Those from affluent countries cannot detach themselves from the needs of the poor and weak.

This agenda on militarism and development is one response to the MWC's call to the churches to confess our disobedience and 'respond to the claims of Christ and His kingdom'. The World Conference challenge requires that North American Mennonites come to terms with ways that our countries, along with other powerful countries, affect the well-being of our neighbors around the world. This paper focuses on the response of people who believe in the biblical message of peace and justice. Specifically it deals with the idolatry of militarism.

Militarism as ideology exalts military values and methods and is used to absolutize loyalty to a social or political system or to guarantee 'national security'. Militarism creates and promotes hostility toward enemies, magnifies threats and hinders conflict resolution. The spirit of militarism instilled in the minds of a civilian population is used to support the absolute demands of a political system. Militarism is most subtle where the production and sale of deadly weapons is accepted as a means of maintaining a thriving economy and an affluent standard of living. Militarism is therefore a form of idolatry long before it expresses itself in specific wars or atrocities.

COMMITMENT TO FAITH

The call to Mennonites of North America is a call to faith and action. Henk B. Kossen of the Netherlands challenged the Mennonite World Conference body in these words:

'What our world needs as much as it needs bread are living peace congregations that by the quality of their community life challenge the rule of the powers, and thereby are able to expose the destructive domination by the powers over society in general, no matter what the consequences. Should such a congregational life come to being, then the Bible must again be central. It must be read and studied in the light of the challenges of this time.'

The way of peace and justice is at the heart of the Christian faith. The essence of historic Mennonite declarations has been that all war and all that contributes to war is sin. This testimony was made practical in the refusal of many Mennonites and others in the United States and Canada to participate in World Wars I and II. Five thousand Canadian Mennonites and five thousand American Mennonites were engaged in constructive civilian work during World War II in place of taking up arms.[1] Conscription was resumed in the U.S. from 1951-1974. Now there is no conscription in our countries. Consequently neither the world nor other Christians hear Mennonites declaring that war is immoral.

The testimony of the churches to the way of peace and justice finds its basis in the biblical witness. On ethical questions and in times of crisis, the church finds the will of God not only through the reading of selected texts, but in the reading of the entire biblical witness.

Mennonites and Brethren in Christ are challenged to recognize that refusal to participate in military service does not in itself counteract contemporary militarism. In Canada and the United States there are today major pressures to preserve and create more jobs in weapons industries by increasing military sales to the Third World. Our economic policies are a clear expression of militarism and must be resisted in the same way that we have traditionally resisted conscription — an expression of militarism we have been able to recognize. Our sincere attempts to serve others in the name of Christ are undermined by our failure to witness against the exploitation of the poor that our arms sales to the Third World represents.

We commend this statement to the Mennonite and Brethren in Christ churches and conferences of the United States and Canada for careful, prayerful attention and encourage them to make resources available for local congregations seeking to deal with the challenge of militarism and the arms race in the last twenty years of this century.

[1] Gingerich, Melvin. *Service for Peace,* Mennonite Central Committee: Akron, PA, 1949.

Adopted by Mennonite Central Committee* - January 27, 1979.

* Mennonite Central Committee is the cooperative relief and service agency of 17 North American Mennonite and Brethren in Christ conferences.

The Response to the Mennonite World Conference

The Mennonite World Conference Tenth Assembly in 1978 offered a clear call to the churches to 'respond to the claims of Christ and his Kingdom.' The Findings Committee report included the call to 'restore our home congregations to Kingdom obedience, to reconcile the broken and the alienated, to seek justice for the oppressed, to witness against powers and principalities who trust in bombs and move toward nuclear holocaust.'

RESOLUTION

Therefore be it resolved that the Mennonite Central Committee calls its supporting churches to reflect on what it means to be people of the Kingdom sharing the good news of the Gospel and its full implications in a broken world. Specific initiatives by MCC and the supporting churches are suggested as follows:

I   To answer the Mennonite World Conference call to 'witness against powers and principalities who trust in bombs and move toward nuclear holocaust':

A. We call upon the supporting churches to work for a moratorium on all military exports and for redirection of resources from production of military weapons to the service of human need.

B. We call upon all people and nations to renounce the research, development, testing, production, deployment and use of nuclear weapons. We call for the conversion of jobs in science and industry from warmaking to peacemaking purposes. Individuals are encouraged to review their industrial employment and investments to make sure they are not contributing unknowingly to the arms race.

II In answer to the Mennonite World Conference call to 'seek justice for the oppressed':

A. We call for new priority to be given to directing world resources to developmental rather than to military purposes. Accordingly, the following activities take on new urgency:

1. Attempts to influence the public policies of the United States and Canada to make more resources available for the service of human need.

2. Expansion of efforts to acquaint the churches of our constituency with the linkages between the economic and military structures of the wealthy countries and needy people in developing countries.

3. Ask selected overseas MCC personnel to study the impact of the arms race on developing countries, and to explore program initiatives that would address the misplacement of priorities in countries where we are working.

III In answer to the Mennonite World Conference call to 'restore our home congregations to Kingdom obedience':

A. We emphasize the importance of sharing the Gospel including the need and opportunity for regeneration through faith in Christ.

B. We urge our churches to become better informed on the circumstances of Christians in other countries which affect their national, economic, and social life and their spiritual wellbeing.

C. We call upon our churches to devote serious attention to the participation of our countries in the arms race, and to the roles of our countries in generating increased military spending in developing countries. We encourage local congregations and conferences to consider and discern ways which they feel are appropriate for them to respond to militarism and the arms race.

D. We call upon our churches and conferences to share these concerns with other Christians, and to give witness to our national governments and others in North America and abroad to the Gospel of Christ and the way of peace.

E. We also call the churches to a way of life that does not depend upon the consumerism and materialism which in some degree perpetuates the militarism we deplore.

A Message from the International Mennonite Peace Committee

Mennonite World Conference, XI Assembly
Strasbourg, July 24 to 29, 1984

INTRODUCTION

This is a brief message from the International Mennonite Peace Committee related to the Mennonite World Conference. We address these words to local Mennonite and Brethren in Christ congregations around the world. We share our analysis and our vision, and invite your counsel. *We invite you to use this statement as a basis for study and action.*

The human family faces staggering problems of malnutrition, hunger, disease, and war. Political and economic powers exploit the human and natural resources of the earth for their own selfish purposes. We in our local churches may not be sure how to respond to these problems, but let us decide to live in solidarity with one another under God. Some of us live under systems that exploit others. Some of us suffer heavy burdens because others exploit us. We are linked with one another. It is appropriate, therefore, that we should ask in our local congregations: 'What is the message of the Gospel for these times?'

We believe that the same Jesus who redeems us is also our peace and our security. The life of Jesus and the message of the Scriptures guide us in our witness to the way of peace and justice. (See the Prophetic writings of the Old Testament; Ephesians 1 to 3; Colossians 2:15; Matthew 5 to 7.)

THE ROLE OF THE CHURCH IN THE NATION

What is the role of the Church in society and among the nations? God has ordained government to order the affairs of society. But God is sovereign and all governments are subject to the authority of God. The Church, as part of the Kingdom of God, witnesses to the will of God for society even if the State is disobedient to the intention of God. There is no place for imposing the will of God on government. But the task of the Church is to create expectations for peace and justice as she witnesses to the Lord of the Kingdom of God. If the Church is silent, how shall the nations know if they are unfaithful to God's mandate? As Takio Tanase of Japan said in our midst, 1 Peter and other Scripture passages direct governments 'to punish those who do wrong and praise those who do right.' The crisis in our time is that some governments persecute those who do right — those who seek freedom to worship and to practice their faith; some governments punish citizens who speak against the ways of violence and oppression.

HUNGER AND THE ARMS RACE

Nations of the earth now rely on military means to stay in power and to solve national and international conflict. They sacrifice the security and the good of their own people so they can have money to buy weapons. Eleven million babies die every year before their first birthday because of malnutrition and disease. Thirty children of the world die every minute because of hunger and sickness. And every minute governments spend 1.3 million dollars for military purposes. The judgment of Isaiah 1:16-17 and Isaiah 10:1-2 speaks to our times:

'Wash yourselves; make yourselves clean; remove the evil of your doings from before my eyes; cease to do evil; learn to do good; seek justice, correct oppression; defend the fatherless, plead for the widow... defend the rights of the needy.'

Surely God's people must call leaders of the world to account for this wicked injustice.

THE THREAT OF NUCLEAR WAR

The threat of nuclear war and the potential nuclear pollution of the environment have been described as the chief moral issues of our time. Nuclear weapons not only kill; they destroy all life. As God's people we serve in hope even in the face of the nuclear threat. So we do not despair. Rather, we witness courageously to the Lord of all creation.

CONCLUSION

Our committee believes that this message is rooted in the evangelistic and ethical vocation of the Church. We confess that we need the reconciling work of God in our local congregations. But let us also join other Christians of East and West, North and South in proclaiming the Word of life in a world of death. Let this sure Word go forth through our churches to 'all nations, for all authority has been given to Jesus who will be with us to the end of the age' (Matthew 28:19-20).

A Covenant for Peace and Justice
(WARC - May, 1983)

A Statement of the Executive Committee
of the World Alliance of Reformed Churches

Introduction

The struggle for peace and justice was a prominent concern of the General Council of the World Alliance of Reformed Churches in Ottawa (August 17-27, 1982). As it dealt with its general theme, 'Thine is the kingdom, the power and the glory,' it was inevitably led to reflect on the forces of hatred, greed and destruction which threaten humanity today. The debate resulted in several statements on peace and justice (Section III, cf. *Reformed World* XXXVII, 3-4, p. 64s., Policy Reference Committee, cf. *Reformed World* XXXVII, 3-4, pp. 69ff., Special Committee on 'Called to Witness to the Gospel Today', pp. 40-47). The concern was again the center of attention when we, the newly elected Executive Committee of the Alliance, came together for our first meeting after the General Council (February 27-March 4, 1983). On the basis of the affirmations made by the General Council we wish to issue the following call.

1. *An imperative of faith*

The General Council left no doubt that the commitment to peace and justice is to be understood as a spiritual obligation. It is demanded by Jesus Christ himself. Therefore, issues of peace and justice do not simply belong to the realm of politics, and must not be decided exclusively on the grounds of pragmatic 'political wisdom'. The General Council emphatically called on the member churches 'to regard the question of peace as not merely a political question, but as one that immediately concerns our commitment to the God of peace' (p. 64). Living with the Gospel implies a constant struggle for the protection of the life which God provides for all humanity and the entire creation. On the basis of this spiritual commitment the Church may be led to contradict established policies of governments and the apparent consensus of society.

2. *Weapons of mass destruction and nuclear war*

Today, the commitment to peace is of the utmost urgency because we are confronted with weapons whose capacity of destruction can lead to the extinction of life. The world lives under the threat of nuclear war. Nobody can be indifferent to this fact.

The General Council called on the churches to engage in a determined and concerted struggle against nuclear armament. It made clear that we are summoned to this struggle by the Gospel itself. 'Insofar as we compromise with evil by supporting the present irrational arms race we are guilty of disobedience to God, and we invite his judgment upon our world. Our attitude towards weapons of mass destruction should be determined by our faith. It is a question of affirming or denying the Gospel itself' (p. 70).

In recent years several Reformed Churches have taken this stand, e.g. the Netherlands Hervormde Kerk. We note that on the issue of nuclear armament a similar consensus is emerging as on the issue of racial discrimination. The Moderamen (Board) of the Reformed Churches in the Federal Republic of Germany went a step further by declaring the 'no' to nuclear arms to be an issue of *status confessionis*. ... 'For us the *status confessionis* is given with it because the attitude taken to means of mass destruction has to do with affirming or denying the Gospel itself.' Several of us feel the use of the term *status confessionis* to be inappropriate in this context but we can accept the statement as a call to renewed witness on this issue. All churches have to see themselves unavoidably challenged to respond to the question of nuclear armament clearly and bindingly as a question of faith and obedience in hearing the Scriptures and praying for the guidance of the Spirit.

What does the struggle against nuclear armament imply for the churches? In our judgment it implies:

— declaring unambiguously that under no circumstances the use of nuclear weapons of any kind can be justified theologically or morally;

— affirming now that no Christian can in good conscience fight for a country which uses nuclear weapons; the attitude of the churches to issues of peace as they arise today must be governed by this affirmation;

— denouncing the folly of the nuclear armament race which increases the risk of nuclear war and consumes resources vitally needed for overcoming the problems of hunger and poverty in today's world;

— making clear that, in the long run, a secure peace cannot be obtained by the strategy of mutual deterrence; though the equilibrium of forces may prevent war for a limited period and may, therefore, serve a purpose at this stage, it does not provide the basis for a longterm solution;

— supporting all genuine efforts at disarmament through multilateral as well as bilateral negotiations;

— inviting the governments of our country to take measures which contribute to building up mutual trust, e.g. renouncing the first use of nuclear weapons or undertaking limited unilateral reduction of the nuclear arms arsenal;

— encouraging movements in our country protesting against the production of nuclear arms, and interpreting their aspirations and demands to the political authorities.

We are aware of the enormous difficulties in translating such an attitude to nuclear arms into political reality. We recognize and share in these difficulties. On the other hand, we are convinced that only on the basis of a determined stand can the political will to find a way out of the impasse and new solutions grow.

3. *Peace and Justice*

Peace is more than the absence of war. Peace means living together as a community in mutual respect, solidarity and justice. Commitment to peace includes, therefore, much more than the struggle against nuclear armament. There is today an acute danger of being exclusively concerned with the horrifying vision of nuclear catastrophe, and of overlooking the other forces which threaten humanity — hunger, poverty, exploitation, discrimination, repression leading inevitably to the violation of fundamental human rights. Above all, we must not forget the many wars which have been conducted in our time with conventional weapons, and have caused the death of millions. Avoiding nuclear conflict, as pressing a task as it is, does not yet mean peace. There is no commitment to peace without an equal commitment to justice. Peace and justice are inseparable.

The General Council pointed particularly to two areas where a renewed commitment is required:

— Peace is threatened by the intolerable injustice of hunger, starvation and poverty. While the gap between the rich and poor nations is increasing, the readiness of the rich nations for sharing their wealth is diminishing. There seems to be a growing acquiescence with the present situation. A new initiative is needed to break the deadlock (*Reformed World* pp. 65 and 70; 'Called to Witness to the Gospel Today', pp. 42-44).

— Peace is threatened by discrimination and repression. If the churches are to serve the cause of peace they need to make their own the cause of human rights. They are summoned by Christ to be present where the dignity of human persons is at stake, especially where fundamental human rights are violated. A movement of protest is required to maintain the protection at least of a minimal core of human rights. As part of this movement the General Council urged the member churches to engage in a campaign against the use of torture (*Reformed World,* pp. 72-74).

4. *A covenant for peace and justice*

On the basis of these considerations we call on the member churches of the Alliance to stand together, and to renew their commitment to peace and justice. Each church needs to bear witness primarily in its own situation, but more and more we must also learn to witness and act together through concerted efforts. At a time when the struggle for peace and justice meets with increasing resistance, and many are tempted to lose heart, we need the witness and encouragement of the churches and Christians of other countries. May the communion in the Alliance increasingly become a source of a common spiritual renewal.

At the same time we dare to propose that all churches which confess Jesus Christ as God and Saviour whatever their tradition should form a covenant for peace and justice. Though they still differ on many issues and cannot yet unite as the one Church of Jesus Christ, they all face the same challenges with regard to peace and justice in the present world. They *can* form a covenant or the particular purpose of a common witness in this field. In order to give visible expression to this covenant, we suggest, under the auspices of the World Council of Churches, the preparation and early summoning of a special ecumenical gathering in which *all* churches would participate and bear witness to ways of peace and justice.

We know that we cannot determine the course of history. The future is not in our hands. God has his own ways of bringing about his kingdom. But as we pray, 'Your kingdom come,' we need to do whatever we can to oppose the destruction of life. As long as we live we are called to be witnesses to God's love for all people and his whole creation.

Contributors

Jean-Marc Chappuis is Professor of Practical Theology at the Theological Faculty of the University of Geneva (address: rue du Mont-de-Sion 4, 1206 Geneva, Switzerland).

Cornelius J. Dyck is Professor of Anabaptist and Sixteenth Century Studies at Associated Mennonite Biblical Seminaries (address: 3003 Benham Avenue, Elkhart, Indiana 46517, USA).

Heinold Fast is pastor of a Mennonite congregation in Emden, West Germany (Address: Brüchstrasse 74, 2970 Emden, Federal Republic of Germany).

Hans Georg vom Berg is pastor of a Reformed parish (address: 3862 Innertkirchen, Bern, Switzerland).

Henk Kossen is Professor of Practical Theology at the Dutch Mennonite Seminary and the University of Amsterdam (address: Albrecht Durerstraat 46-II P.c., 1077 MB Amsterdam, Netherlands).

Larry Miller is Director of Peace and Interchurch Relations for the European Office of the Mennonite Central Committee (address: 27, rue des Jardiniers, 67000 Strasbourg, France).

Ernst Saxer is Professor of Church History on the Evangelical Faculty at the University of Bern (address: Casinostrasse 6, 8600 Dübendorf, Switzerland).

Alan Sell is Theological Secretary of the World Alliance of Reformed Churches (address: 150, rte de Ferney, Box 66, 1211 Geneva 20, Switzerland).

Lukas Vischer is Professor of Ecumenical Theology at the University of Bern and Moderator of the Theology Department of the World Alliance of Reformed Churches (address: Sulgenauweg 26, 3000 Bern 23, Switzerland).

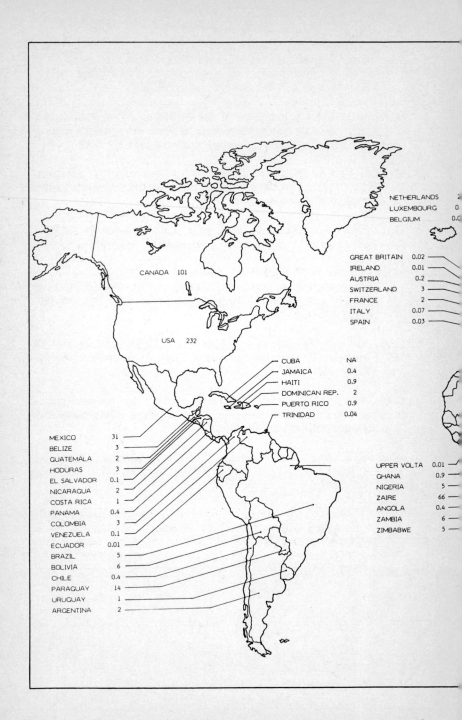

NETHERLANDS   2
LUXEMBOURG   0
BELGIUM   0.0

GREAT BRITAIN   0.02
IRELAND   0.01
AUSTRIA   0.2
SWITZERLAND   3
FRANCE   2
ITALY   0.07
SPAIN   0.03

CANADA   101

USA   232

CUBA   NA
JAMAICA   0.4
HAITI   0.9
DOMINICAN REP.   2
PUERTO RICO   0.9
TRINIDAD   0.04

MEXICO   31
BELIZE   3
GUATEMALA   2
HODURAS   3
EL SALVADOR   0.1
NICARAGUA   2
COSTA RICA   1
PANAMA   0.4
COLOMBIA   3
VENEZUELA   0.1
ECUADOR   0.01
BRAZIL   5
BOLIVIA   6
CHILE   0.4
PARAGUAY   14
URUGUAY   1
ARGENTINA   2

UPPER VOLTA   0.01
GHANA   0.9
NIGERIA   5
ZAIRE   66
ANGOLA   0.4
ZAMBIA   6
ZIMBABWE   5

MENNONITE WORLD MEMBERSHIP MAP

Membership by country in thousands (e.g. 0.9 = 900 members)

USSR	55
GERMAN DEM. REP.	0.2
FED. REP. OF GERMANY	12

JAPAN	3
TAIWAN	1
HONG KONG	0.03
PHILIPPINES	3
VIETNAM	0.2

INDIA   44

ETHIOPIA	7
SOMALIA	0.1
KENYA	3
TANZANIA	14

INDONESIA   63

AUSTRALIA   0.01

(1984)

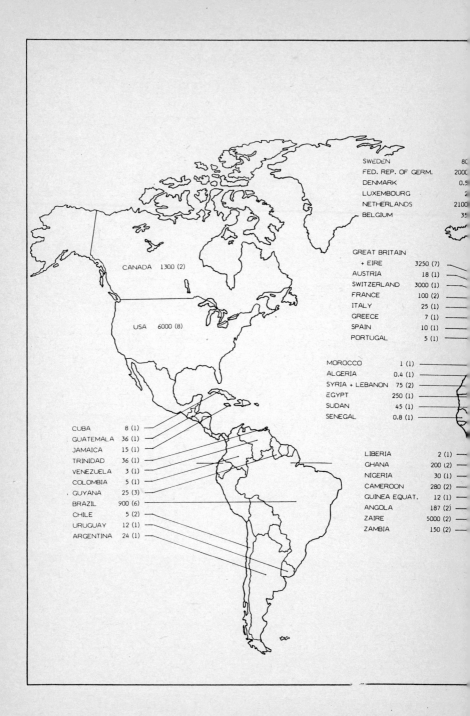

SWEDEN   80
FED. REP. OF GERM. 2000
DENMARK   0.5
LUXEMBOURG   2
NETHERLANDS   2100
BELGIUM   35

GREAT BRITAIN
+ EIRE   3250 (7)
AUSTRIA   18 (1)
SWITZERLAND   3000 (1)
FRANCE   100 (2)
ITALY   25 (1)
GREECE   7 (1)
SPAIN   10 (1)
PORTUGAL   5 (1)

MOROCCO   1 (1)
ALGERIA   0.4 (1)
SYRIA + LEBANON   75 (2)
EGYPT   250 (1)
SUDAN   45 (1)
SENEGAL   0.8 (1)

CANADA   1300 (2)

USA   6000 (8)

CUBA   8 (1)
GUATEMALA   36 (1)
JAMAICA   15 (1)
TRINIDAD   36 (1)
VENEZUELA   3 (1)
COLOMBIA   5 (1)
GUYANA   25 (3)
BRAZIL   900 (6)
CHILE   5 (2)
URUGUAY   12 (1)
ARGENTINA   24 (1)

LIBERIA   2 (1)
GHANA   200 (2)
NIGERIA   30 (1)
CAMEROON   280 (2)
GUINEA EQUAT.   12 (1)
ANGOLA   187 (2)
ZAIRE   5000 (2)
ZAMBIA   150 (2)

WORLD ALLIANCE OF REFORMED CHURCHES
MEMBERSHIP MAP

Membership by country in thousands and number of member churches
(e.g. Angola 187 (2) = 187,000 members, 2 member churches)

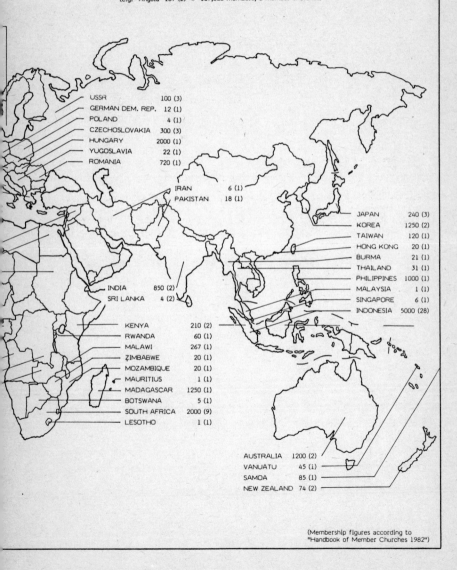

USSR	100 (3)
GERMAN DEM. REP.	12 (1)
POLAND	4 (1)
CZECHOSLOVAKIA	300 (3)
HUNGARY	2000 (1)
YUGOSLAVIA	22 (1)
ROMANIA	720 (1)

IRAN	6 (1)
PAKISTAN	18 (1)

JAPAN	240 (3)
KOREA	1250 (2)
TAIWAN	120 (1)
HONG KONG	20 (1)
BURMA	21 (1)
THAILAND	31 (1)
PHILIPPINES	1000 (1)
MALAYSIA	1 (1)
SINGAPORE	6 (1)
INDONESIA	5000 (28)

INDIA	850 (2)
SRI LANKA	4 (2)

KENYA	210 (2)
RWANDA	60 (1)
MALAWI	267 (1)
ZIMBABWE	20 (1)
MOZAMBIQUE	20 (1)
MAURITIUS	1 (1)
MADAGASCAR	1250 (1)
BOTSWANA	5 (1)
SOUTH AFRICA	2000 (9)
LESOTHO	1 (1)

AUSTRALIA	1200 (2)
VANUATU	45 (1)
SAMOA	85 (1)
NEW ZEALAND	74 (2)

(Membership figures according to
"Handbook of Member Churches 1982")

Geneva and Lombard, 1986